DISSERTATION
COMPLETION GUIDE

A Chapter-by-Chapter Nontechnical Guide
for Graduate Research Projects

DANIEL S. ALEMU, PHD

Proficient Professionals Group, LLC
Latham, NY

Library of Congress Cataloging-in-Publication Data

ISBN-10:0-692-70119-2
ISBN-13:978-0-692-70119-5

Contents

Acknowledgements

I gratefully acknowledge my colleagues Dr. Robert Bradley of The Sage Colleges and Dr. Michael Abebe of The University of Texas Rio Grande Valley for their constructive comments.

About the Author

Dr. Daniel S. Alemu received his PhD from Illinois State University. Currently, he is a full-time tenured associate professor at the Sage Colleges, in Troy/Albany, New York. He teaches doctoral-level research-methods courses in the department of educational leadership, where he is also the director of doctoral research. Dr. Alemu has served in numerous doctoral dissertation committees and chaired more than twenty five successfully defended dissertations. His publications, on various issues, appeared in internationally and nationally circulated peer-reviewed journals including *International Review of Education* , *Kappa Delta Pi Record*, *Journal for Effective Schools*, and *Planning and Changing Journal*. He also presented his research in professional conferences, including at AERA, NCPEA, UCEA, and MWERA to mention some.

Preface

Completing a graduate program often requires, at least partially, writing a research thesis or conducting some kind of culminating or capstone project. Doctoral programs, by design, are research oriented, and candidates in such programs are expected to effectively use research-based studies and to be able to independently produce their own research/dissertation. For the candidates, writing a dissertation is the most challenging aspect of all the requirements of the doctoral program.

The challenge stems from various reasons. First, it requires the individual candidate to possess a whole gamut of research skills and sufficient knowledge of the research topic. Second, for most candidates, writing a dissertation is the first experience of conducting standard, original research. Third, conducting doctoral research is an independent process starting from formulating the research problem to conducting the actual research and reporting the findings.

Graduate programs traditionally prepare candidates to complete their theses through offering research-methods seminars and assigning research advisors. However, a good number of students still struggle through the process. There is an undeniably wide gap between what the candidates need to successfully finish their dissertations and what graduate programs provide to prepare candidates to independently perform the task.

The most commonly observed reasons for the creation of this gap include one or more of the following. First, courses that are intended to prepare graduate students to complete their research/dissertations end up being either overwhelming or underwhelming depending on the rigor of the curriculum, the orientation of the college (teaching versus research), the teaching philosophy and capability of the instructor, the research background of the student, or a combination of these. The second reason is lack of clear standards and expectations about dissertation. There is no such thing as a standard dissertation manual uniform to all colleges. Where there are institutional manuals, they provide the basics of what should be followed such as the formats, writing style, and the defense process. The students are often left without a reasonable guidance on the details of their work. Third, there is a very ambiguous definition of *independent* task. Some faculty members or institutions may discourage individual candidates from seeking help on essential dissertation-related issues, because they think "the student is supposed to know all at this level" or this is something "the student should learn on his or her own through the process"— leaving the student practically in a sink-or-swim situation. Finally, for some candidates, some jargon or technical terms of the graduate research process are factors learned while doing the actual research. The learning curve is sharp and at times short.

This is not to suggest that all candidates in doctoral programs could graduate if these problems are solved. However, the following staggeringly low doctoral-study completion rate could be improved.

According to a ten-year study of doctoral-study completion from the 1992–93 to 2003–04 academic years, the Council for Graduate Schools (2008) reports doctoral completion rates to be 55 percent for women and 58 percent for men. Completion also varies by academic fields. According to the same study, the completion rate for women engineering majors was 56 percent, compared to their male counterparts (65 percent). In life science the rate was 56 percent for women and 64 percent for men; in social sciences it was 57 percent for women and 53 percent for men. And in humanities the rate was the lowest, at 52 percent for women and 47 percent for men completion.

What happens when candidates fail to graduate with their cohorts/class varies by individual candidate's decisions and institutional policy regarding completion timeline. For the most part, higher education institutions in the United States require candidates to complete their doctoral study in a specific time set by the institutions. This leaves a good number of such struggling candidates as ABD (All But Dissertation) for years or forever, partly due to disorientation in the research process that emanated from one or more of the earlier-mentioned problems.

Disorientation in the research process may lead some candidates to take steps out of desperation. In good instances, they may be able to get guidance outside of the formal channel and finish without compromising the ethical expectation of academic integrity. In bad instances, candidates may be subjected to register and pay for dissertation hours year after year with the hope that they will finish one day. In the worst case, candidates may end up in unethical situation of academic dishonesty. It is an open secret that the web is not free from predators seeking to prey on the vulnerable, including the struggling dissertators. Some candidates could be misled or lured by individuals or organizations that advertise in such a way that they will provide with a completed proposal or a finished dissertation and find themselves in an illegal and unethical situation.

This guide is designed to provide graduate students with an alternative resource, supplemental to what their institutions offer. It is not a research-methods book. This guide doesn't substitute for any research-methods course either. Research-methods books and courses in quantitative and qualitative research are essential to complete parts of chapters 3 and 4 of a dissertation. This author, after teaching research-methods courses in a doctoral program for over eight years and after advising over twenty five successfully defended dissertations, is convinced of the need for a nontechnical guide that encompasses all dissertation chapters. This book is, therefore, designed to help mitigate disorientations in the research process by guiding candidates chapter by chapter.

Organization of the Book

This book is organized in a user-friendly manner that any person in a doctoral or graduate-level program who is required to write a research document will find helpful. It is organized in three parts.

Part 1 follows the commonly used five-chapter dissertation format in education and the social sciences and explains specific components to be included in each chapter. It also elaborates the technical aspects of each chapter.

Part 2 gives guidance in designing and pilot testing data-collection tools and instruments. It also provides sample questionnaire, interview protocols, and observation instruments.

Part 3 focuses on common research terminologies and concepts helpful to any novice researcher. At the end, the appendices section provides some useful resource as well.

Part 1: Components of a Dissertation

This section is organized mirroring a commonly used five-chapter dissertation in education and the social sciences. The first chapter covers the introduction chapter of a dissertation. Chapter 2 discusses literature review. Chapters 3 and 4 cover methodology and data analysis, respectively. Finally, chapter 5 discusses summary of findings, conclusions, and recommendations.

Each chapter provides explanations of the chapter followed by specific components that should be included in the chapter. When possible, examples are provided to help readers easily understand the concepts and contents covered.

Introduction (Chapter 1)

Before extensively discussing the detail components of the first chapter (Introduction) of a dissertation, it is imperative to provide a context of what chapter 1 is in the first place.

All about the Introductory Chapter

As in any formal document, the introduction introduces the entire work in a nutshell. The introduction part of a dissertation is one of the major chapters organized in such a way that it provides a foundation to the entire research work by addressing several interrelated subtopics item by item. It provides an overview of the problem to be investigated to the readers. It lays the background by summarizing theories and seminal works done in the aspect of the problem to be studied. It justifies the need for conducting the research, provides the framework for the study, and describes the potential benefits of the final product, thereby clearly familiarizing the reader what to expect throughout the document.

While some aspect of the introduction of a dissertation develops through the research process, it is a requirement that a candidate in most traditional and nontraditional terminal-degree-offering institutions must write prior to formally starting the research.

In other words, it is part of both the research proposal to be approved (usually by dissertation committee members) and part of the final research document. In some institutions, the research proposal constitutes the first three chapters (Introduction, Literature Review, and Research Methodology), while in others, it constitutes only some parts of these chapters. Either way, the introduction chapter is the place for the researcher to convince not only his or her research committee but also to the readers at large about the need and the manner in which the research is conducted.

Hence, the candidate needs to put a concerted effort in writing the introduction in a manner commensurate with what it deserves. There is rarely a second chance for first impression. The first chapter is the first impression for the candidate!

The commonly used components/templates of the introductory chapter of a dissertation are discussed with examples in the next section.

Background/Overview of the Study

The first subsection of chapter 1 provides background or overview of the study. In this section, the candidate is expected to present all about the area of the study. The researcher describes the problem by providing evidence from prior seminal studies about the topic in a very general or global manner.

This is not the place to talk about the candidate's specific study. It is a section where the background of what is to be studied is provided along with the context supported by previous works. In short, the candidate explains what the area of study is and why the topic is important.

Example: Let's say a candidate wanted to investigate the reasons behind high turnover of middle-school principals in New York City, and he or she phrased the title as "Determinants of Middle-School Principals' Turnover in New York City."

The candidate's job is to provide what makes turnover an important problem to be studied and what prior studies suggested or concluded based on their findings. While chapter 2 is entirely dedicated to a literature review, the researcher also needs to reference the nuggets of relevant prior works about the topic here. Using our example, a good writer starts with a broader explanation about turnover but quickly narrows the focus on the issue (turnover) as it relates to educational leaders in general and school principals in specific. Unless the selected topic is a new field of study or understudied, researchers don't have to include literature beyond their field of study. In addition, although the broader area is "turnover," it doesn't make sense to provide in the background unrelated "turnover" issues such as "turnover of astronauts" or "high turnover of nannies in New York City" and the like.

The background/overview part is concluded by underlining or providing a summarized analysis of what prior studies addressed and did not address—meaning the gap between what has been studied regarding the problem or issue and what has not been studied. The gap could be a list of areas or issues that are not well addressed in the grand research area, of which the proposed study is one. For example, based on his or her reading of the seminal works on school principals, the researcher may conclude the following:

Although there is a great deal of study on issues of principal turnover in more global and national contexts, very little is studied about middle-school principals in general and urban principals in specific. There is also little research that focused on New York City principal turnover. More importantly, much of the research on the issue of principal turnover was conducted over two decades ago, thereby necessitating the need for further research that shows the current trend.

This will logically transition us to the next section: Statement of the Problem.

Statement of the Problem

The last part of the previous section should give a very smooth and logical transition to write a focused statement of the problem. This is the section where the researcher justifies his or her research. What is to be studied? Why is it relevant? And why now?

The candidate may start this section by indicating the research gap in prior studies about the issue of interest and what the proposed study addresses. Using our prior example, the researcher may briefly indicate what prior studies didn't address that the current research is going to address regarding the issue of "turnover" and more specifically "turnover of middle-school principals in New York City."

It is not enough to mention the observed gap. The researcher needs to justify that the gap observed is worth studying. What needs to be explained here is simply what motivates the researcher to think about and conduct this research by presenting arguments in a scholarly manner and by supporting the claims with data when possible. Using our example, if what motivates the researcher to conduct the study is a reported/observed "high turnover of principals in New York City middle schools," evidence or data that supports the claim from published reports, official documents, or relevant studies that can be referenced should be presented. How high and how pervasive the observed turnover should also be well argued.

Once the researcher exhausted the rationale for conducting the research, the last paragraph of this section presents the research *purpose statement*.

Purpose statement, according to Creswell (2009), is "the intent of the entire research study" (p.111), and it sets "the objective, intent, or major idea" (p.112). In short, it is a declaration of what is to be done in a very clear and unambiguous manner. Generally, a purpose statement is presented in the form of a paragraph addressing such areas as:

- What (What is the study all about/the central phenomenon to be explored, including study variables when appropriate)?
- Where (Where is the research site)?
- Who (Who are the research participants/focus of the study)?
- How (How is it designed? Is it quantitative, qualitative, or mixed)?

Theoretical/Conceptual Framework

Almost always, there is at least one underlying theory/structured idea that guides how we see or approach things. Theory is simply defined as "a statement of relationships between units observed or approximated in the empirical world" (Bacharach, 1989, p.498). Good theories, according to Bacharach, address the how, when, and why of variables. Theory is especially a critical component of quantitative research design that intends to test models or conventionally accepted thinking.

By taking the prior example of middle-school principal turnover, through reading prior studies on the issue, one may come across various models/theories about the issue of turnover such as the causal model, push-pull model, fit-misfit model, factual-perceptual model, met expectations model, and so forth.

Just to give you an example, the *push-pull model* as it applies to employee turnover may be written as follows:

The theoretical framework used for this study is the push-pull model. Having its root in global labor migration, the push-pull theory stipulates that for people to leave their organization for a new destination, several push and pull factors should involve. Applied in turnover studies, the push factors are unfavorable (negative) factors associated with the original work place that drive individuals away and the pull factors are favorable (positive) factors that attract individuals to the new place of employment. The push factors simply include negative experiences of individual employees such as poor treatment, low compensation, absence of growth opportunities, bad work environment and so on. The pull factors on the other hand include such perceived favorable conditions as good work environment, better pay, better treatment, availability of various opportunities and the like in the new place of employment.

The researcher, at least, has to explain how the issue had been studied and theorized in the past and how he or she is going to address the issue based on the proposed models/theories. The researcher may either use formerly developed theories or propose a new theoretical framework based on conceptualizing the issue as a result of his or her comprehensive understanding of previous studies and literature on the issue supported by rich experience in the field.

No one is expected to know all the theoretical frameworks or models about the issue of interest. In some field of studies, there are almost as many theories as the number of writers on the issue. However, a targeted, exhaustive familiarization on published relevant theories is essential.

Such familiarization helps one not to overlook commonly known theories about the topic or issue. Second, it helps the researcher not to waste time in trying to do what has already been effectively addressed in the past. Third, it helps to tell the readers that the researcher is well read about the topic, thereby adding credibility to the study. And finally, it helps the researcher to have a concept map of what his or her research is all about and how it is to be approached in a vivid manner.

Research Questions and Hypotheses

After discussing the statement of the problem and conceptual framework, what come logically are the research questions that address the topic in a specific manner. Research questions/hypothesis provide specific focus about what is to be inquired. They provide the road map to base the entire research work including but not limited to the literature review, the survey/interview questions, and the research methodology. In short, the purpose of the entire research document is to answer the research questions/hypotheses the researcher attempts to answer. Usually, in a dissertation, the researcher presents two to five basic research questions/hypothesis that specifically address the topic of inquiry.

Research questions are presented in the form of questions in general. The manner the questions are framed differ in some ways between quantitative and qualitative research designs. Qualitative questions usually, but not always, ask the "how," while quantitative research is more likely to ask the "what." Taking the same example about principal turnover, a qualitative research question may look like:

How does school climate contribute to middle schools principals' turnover?

Whereas a quantitative research question may look like:

What relationship, if any, exists between middle-school principal turnover and school climate?

While research questions are used in qualitative, quantitative, and mixed-method studies, research hypothesis is exclusively for quantitative research designs aimed at significance testing.

A research hypothesis is often presented in two ways. It is first stated as an empirically testable statement based on logic or the researcher's assumption and past research findings. But, it is also stated as in an opposite way from what the researcher speculates known as the "null hypothesis." Taking our prior example of principal turnover, the researcher might hypothesize that:

Hypothesis (H1): There is a relationship between middle-school principal turnover and school climate.

Null Hypothesis (H0): There is no relationship between middle-school principal turnover and school climate.

The idea is that if the test/experiment results in supporting the researcher's claim in the end, then the "Null Hypothesis" is rejected, thereby showing the significance of the result of the experiment.

Significance of the Study

It is not only customary but also very important that the researcher states the significance of the study in the first chapter. Research is conducted with certain beneficiaries in mind; thus, the researcher should thoroughly think and explain in a clear manner about who will benefit from the research he or she is conducting and in what way.

In short, if you should give the finished document to people/institutions that you think would benefit from your study the most, who will you give it to? And why? This section needs to answer these. It is helpful to think in terms of individuals, groups, or institutions that have a direct or indirect connection or association with the topic and the geographical location, and the scope of the study. Taking the prior example of middle-school principal turnover, one may think about significance in terms of policy and practice related to the issue.

Thus, a researcher may think thoroughly about the issue as it relates to the hiring and retention practices and policies of principals by the school districts or the department of education (DOE), principal preparation and orientation process, awareness on the connections between the climate of the schools and turnover, and on the impact of principal turnover on the teachers, students, and the school community in general. Then the researcher should clearly state how these policies and practices benefit the intended beneficiaries.

Definition of Terms/Keywords

Not all terms we use in our research convey the same meaning and interpretation by all of our readers. This usually gets worse if we use so much jargon because of the nature of the research.

The researcher, thus, should provide definitions of some technical/operational terms selectively. It should be understood that the objective of defining the terms is not to make the document easily understood by lay persons to the field. If readers are not familiar to the general area of your study, defining the terms alone makes no difference in their understanding of the subject. The goal in defining technical terms should rather be to minimize confusion on the use of the terms that, if not well defined, would give different meaning to different people.

One of the dilemmas a researcher faces in relation to defining terms is the level of detail to be included. Here are a few tips: If possible, define the term in one sentence. Use sources when applicable such as government documents, relevant literature, research documents, and so forth. But if there is a need for the researcher to coin his or her own technical definition, it is possible as well. The point is to minimize confusion by providing the meaning of the term as applied in the study.

Using our prior example, let's say the researcher wanted to define *high turnover of principals*. The purpose here is to help readers to understand what turnover means in terms of its intensity, such as how high is "high." The definition may look like this:

High Principal Turnover: The frequency of principals leaving a school within two or less years of their hire.

A similar study may suggest the frequency to be within a year or within three years. What matters is how the term is used in the study. It should, thus, be defined accordingly.

Scope of the Study

The scope of the study section (also known as "delimitation") is where the boundary of the research is explained using clear criteria or parameters as set by the researcher.

Depending on the type of the research, boundaries are usually set in terms of place (the geographical location/setting of the study), participants of the study (the characteristics of individuals from whom data are collected and/or about whom conclusion will be reached), and the time (the specific timeline when the data will be collected). The parameters may involve other criteria such as the focus of the study and the type of data-collection instruments or tools.

Because the research methodology chapter more or less covers aspects of the scope of the study, dissertation formats in recent years have not been consistent in including this subsection in their chapter 1. The inclusion or exclusion of this subsection varies from university to university and from research committee to research committee.

Limitation of the Study

This is the place where the researcher states the problems related to conducting the research. In other words, this is where the researcher states what did not go as planned or unforeseen issues with conducting the research.

Although "Limitation of the Study" is usually part of chapter 1, some institutions prefer it toward the end of the last chapter. In any case, it is written after the study has been completed. This is because, the researcher cannot talk about problems encountered in the process before going through the process.

If the researcher writes "limitations" before the research is conducted, what this practically means is that the researcher is telling his or her audience that "I knew this problem would impact the study but I studied it anyway." This implies negligence not limitation. In short, the researcher needs to document unanticipated constraints rather than her/his "plan for disaster."

The researcher should try to foresee potential problems and plan for success. However, no matter how well one plans, things may *not* go as planned. The future is always uncertain. This unpredictability comes in many forms. One of the potential interviewees may step down of her positions, or natural disaster may occur that affects the study. We cannot possibly prepare ahead of time for such things. The researcher needs to document and list problems that in one way or another affected the study to provide readers with enough background and justifications of why the study had not been conducted exactly as planned.

Organization of the Study

The "Organization of the Study" subsection of chapter 1 is where the researcher explains how the dissertation is organized, such as how many chapters the dissertation has and what each chapter contains. This is very important at least for two reasons.

First, higher education institutions use different dissertation formats. The researcher has to describe the format here if it is, for example, a five- or six-chapter format or so. Second, what is stated in each chapter is affected by the format; hence, the researcher needs to describe what each chapter contains.

Here is an example:

This dissertation is organized in five chapters. Chapter 1 introduces the research and provides the background for the study. Chapter 2 presents the literature review relevant to the study. Chapter 3 explains the research methodology and specific procedures followed to conduct the study. Chapter 4 presents data analysis. The last chapter provides summary of findings, conclusions, and recommendations.

Final Note: Most colleges provide outlines of what should be included in chapter 1 of the doctoral dissertation. Commonly, this is included in the research handbook of the appropriate graduate program/school. It is also expected that individual research committee chair or committee members provide some specific direction or set their expectation of what the chapter should and shouldn't include. The candidate is strongly encouraged to follow those specific outlines and directions.

Literature Review (Chapter 2)

Chapter 2 of the commonly used dissertation model documents the literature review. In this guide, points that are relevant to write an effective literature review are emphasized. The first one is explanation of the meaning of literature review. The second one addresses the purpose of literature review. Then, a framework on what should be included in the literature review in terms of content is presented. Finally, tips on resources that will help in writing scholarly document are provided.

What is a Literature Review?

While this looks a very elementary question, the change in higher education curriculum offerings in recent years is compelling enough to include this subtopic in this guide. In the past, thesis writing was, at least, a partial graduation requirement in graduate programs. Even, in some cases, undergraduate students were required to complete senior essays to graduate, where a literature review was part of the document. In recent years, however, institutions offer a nonthesis option for graduation that many students incline to choose. As a result, it is highly likely that a good number of terminal-degree seekers or doctoral students in today's higher education come with very limited preparation to write their dissertation, in general, and complete their literature review, in particular.

A literature review, according to Machi and McEvoy (2009, p.4), is "a written document that presents a logically argued case founded on a comprehensive understanding of the current state of knowledge about a topic of study. This case establishes a convincing thesis to answer the study's question." Similarly, Fink (2010, p.3) explains that "a research literature review is a systematic, explicit, and reproducible method for identifying, evaluating, and synthesizing the existing body of completed and recorded work produced by researchers, scholars, and practitioners."

In a simple way, a literature review, in a dissertation, is a written document the candidate prepares based on what has been written about, regarding the topic of interest or the area of the study. It starts by identifying literature about the topic followed by documenting relevant works, sifting the more important from the less important ones, and culminating with writing a synthesized and refined chapter on what prior works/findings say about the topic.

The Purpose and Benefits of Literature Review

A literature review provides a comprehensive analysis of prior studies on the issue/problem. It should be noted that while a literature review is the second chapter in a formal research document, it is the first thing a researcher does in conducting a research.

Asking why we need a literature review is the same as asking why we need to know what prior studies found or suggested about the topic of interest. Multiple possible answers justify why we need literature review as part of a dissertation document.

First, it familiarizes the researcher with the body of work written about the topic/subject and helps/enables him or her to shape a potential research topic. A researcher may come up with a potential topic due to various background reasons or motivations such as observation of a problem that commanded his or her attention, a desire to solve a problem he or she or society faces, a vision for creating a new way of doing things, a felt need to record or document history in a scholarly manner, to prove or disprove theories, or even out of curiosity. Without an effort for deeper understanding of the problem through reviewing relevant literature, the researcher may not be successful in coming up with a good research topic.

Through the process of conducting the literature review, the researcher not only understands the problem better but also becomes familiar with seminal work on the issue and gets a sense of authorities on the subject and recent debates/development about the issue in general.

In higher education, doctoral candidates work with their research advisor, the dissertation chair, to refine the potential topic. A good research advisor usually advises the candidate to familiarize him- or herself with the body of research around the potential topic from the get go.

Second, as a result of reading previous studies around the potential topic, the researcher will have a better sense of what has been and what has not been studied. Understanding what has been studied and what has not been studied in return will have two advantages. Primarily, it helps the researcher to frame a workable topic, to come up with good potential research questions, and to design a quality questionnaire or interview items. It also saves the researcher from wasting time and energy in trying to conduct a research that has been already extensively studied or as the saying goes—it saves the novice researcher from "kicking the dead horse."

Third, writing a good literature review will benefit the researcher in writing a good research report. Although literature review is formally put as chapter 2, its benefit to the researcher goes beyond understanding what has been studied. It guides the researcher to see his or her final research findings in light of previous works and studies. A good research report provides analysis taking into account the convergence and divergence of findings to relevant studies in the past.

Fourth, a good literature review provides credibility about the researcher by giving a reasonable sense to the dissertation committee members and the readers in general that the researcher is well read and has built his or her work on previous seminal works.

Finally, although writing a comprehensive literature review for a dissertation is the first experience for most candidates, it is highly possible that the researcher will continue writing literature review in the future, depending on the researcher's career path. Almost all academic documents including publishing articles, presenting in academic forums such as conferences and seminars, submitting grant

proposals, and the like will have a literature review component.
Writing a dissertation literature review is thus a benefit not only to complete the doctoral-study requirements but also to future professional obligations.

A Framework on Where to Start and What to Include

As discussed earlier, familiarization about the topic of interest is one of the things that a researcher should do in the process of writing a research document. The process of familiarization may have four potential steps.

The first step is accessing library database to search for literature on the area of interest in general. The second step is selecting *relevant* literature from a possible long list of published work. And the third one is compiling an annotated bibliography. The fourth step is writing a synthesized literature review in a coherent and seamless manner guided by the general topic, organized in meaningful subsections, and addressing contents related to specific areas of inquiry covered in each research question.

Accessing a Library/Research Database. While some fields are extensively studied, others are not so. Many issues in social sciences and humanities, for example, are extensively studied that researchers have little challenge finding relevant literature, be it electronic or classic hard copies. On the contrary, some new/emerging fields of study, like technology and the social media for example, may not be as well exhaustively studied as other fields to easily search and find rich research database.

In any case, accessing a research or library database has never been easier as now, where we can easily generate a rich list of literature with a tip of our finger by clicking mouse or tapping a touch screen, using a key word/phrase, and storing them in a tiny flash drive (and even better, storing them in a remote server or *cloud*).

A good place to start the literature search in the area of interest is the library. Higher education institutions usually assign individual librarians for specific fields of studies who can help with a wide variety of questions the users may have. It is wise to contact a librarian assigned to areas of your interest as early as possible.

Libraries of higher education institutions usually have a long list of a database of publications either by the name of the providers or by the fields of study. Some of these databases are rich both in the quality and quantity of the documents they carry, while others may not be as rich depending on the preference and the resources of the institutions.

While electronic database are becoming increasingly popular among users, libraries carry large collections of print and audiovisual resources as well. Among the common electronic databases higher education institutions carry, in education and social sciences, include ProQuest, ERIC, EBSCO HOST, and WorldCat. While sites like Google scholar and other open access journals carry valuable resources, it is imperative that the researcher puts extra caution about resources from the World Wide Web.

Depending on the nature of the topic or the field of study or the search phrase/criteria used, one may end up with either a very few or an endless list of studies/documents. The question is how to select the relevant ones from those that have less or no relevance to the specific topic of interest.

Selecting Relevant Resources for Literature Review. It is unrealistic to expect any person, whether a novice or seasoned researcher, to read all published and unpublished works to choose what is relevant and what is not relevant in the area of interest. The following five steps to selecting relevant literature from a long list of materials and documents written about the topic may help:

Step 1: Title checking. Depending on the search criteria (word or phrases) used, some of the resources or journal articles may be more related to your topic than others. Taking our prior example, let's say we used *principals turnover* as a key phrase to search in ProQuest database. The search generated 201,801 search results as seen below:

Figure 1. Initial search

It is obvious that this long list can be narrowed by changing or rephrasing the key phrase. Just by adding one word *school* and putting the phrase in quotation mark as "School principal turnover," the list in the search has been significantly reduced to just eleven as seen below in figure 2.

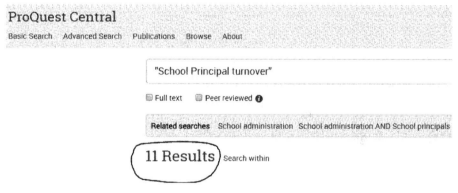

Figure 2. Narrowed search

In addition, by selecting/checking the "Full Text" and "Peer Reviewed" boxes, a fewer relevant list can be populated. The titles of the first five, using our narrowed search, are presented in figure 3.

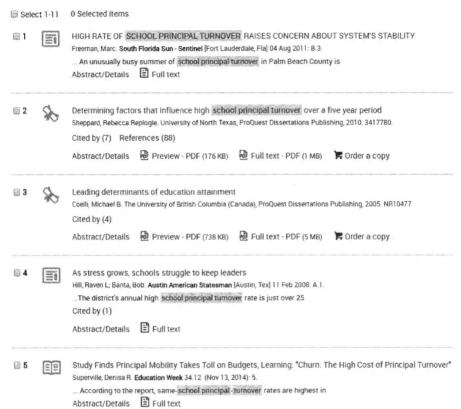

Figure 3. Sample list of resources

Through *Title Checking* one can easily understand that not all that show in the search list are equally relevant documents to the study.

The researcher needs to screen the list further by adding alternative words or phrases such as "departure" or "mobility" in place of *turnover* and by narrowing the screening criteria such as limiting to "full text" and "peer reviewed."

Step 2: Journal/source screening. Not all resources that we get even in a widely accepted database have equal weight or relevance. In a literature review, research-based studies are more preferred than some books and opinion pieces. Even from research-based studies, those studies that passed through multiple reviewers before being published, commonly known as peer reviewed or refereed, are reputable. Most electronic library databases have online search criteria that allow researchers to easily select peer-reviewed ones as figure 1 above shows.

Occasionally, depending on the nature of the study and the scarcity or availability of resources on a topic, the researcher may go beyond peer-reviewed journals and books. Government documents, for example, can be helpful if related to the topic. It is always good to have consultation with your dissertation chair whenever a non-research-based document is of interest to you, because he or she is in a better position and more experienced to judge the exhaustiveness of your search for peer-reviewed and research-based publications.

In addition, while there is a debate about whether dissertations are peer-reviewed documents or not, and that your search engine might not identify it as peer reviewed, it is a common practice to use a few well-written dissertations as a literature review resource as well.

Step 3: Abstract and table of content scanning. Once we find a list of publications to be relevant in terms of title and source, the next thing to do is going through the abstract or the table of content of books. It is a standard requirement for journal articles to have an abstract that briefly explains what the study is about and how it is conducted and possibly highlights the major findings. Reading the abstract or scanning through the book's table of contents gives a sense whether the article or book is worth reading in detail or not, thereby narrowing the list to the more relevant ones.

Step 4: Content evaluation. Abstracts or table of contents do not tell us all. Some articles with a well-written abstract may end up being poor in terms of content. Because abstracts are mostly written in a generalized manner, relying on them to judge the quality of the work is like "judging the book by its cover." Scanning the articles and books page by page, going deeper to look further into the content of the study, helps the researcher to sift the relevant from the potential long list.

Step 5: Compiling annotated bibliography. After completing content evaluation and narrowing the list into more relevant literature to the study, the next step is to do an annotated bibliography.

An annotated bibliography describes documents in terms of three attributes: (a) bibliographical information (author, year of publication, title, type of document, etc); (b) objective summary (evaluative by nature) of the document in terms of its relevance to the study;

and (c) note or reflective rating by the researcher about the quality (rigor, methodology, result/findings) of the research/document (for example, as "critical/must be included," "should be used," or "may be used," etc.).

In addition, compiling the annotated bibliography will provide the researcher with clearer information about the authors and publishers that frequently publish about the topic of interest. This is typically important, in case the researcher wants to contact authors later in the process in relation to the study, for example, the researcher may want to contact the authors if there is a need to use the instruments such as questionnaires or interview protocols that they used.

Writing the Literature Review

Once prior literature are compiled, annotated, and sorted out by their relevance in terms of content, methodology, and result, the next step will be writing the literature review. At this point, the researcher may ask such logical questions as: where to start, what to focus on, and which resources to use where and when?

Where to begin? Although there is no one best way of doing the literature review, starting with outlining is usually very helpful. Outlining strategies may differ by individual preferences or even by the nature of the study. There are three common ways of outlining and organizing literature review: chronological, methodological, and thematic.

As the name suggests, chronological outlining helps to organize by events/time. When using methodological outlining, the researcher follows a certain contextual order of organizing as it makes sense to the researcher and fits the subject studied. Thematic outlining is used when outlining is made by breaking the grand research of interest into smaller subcomponents or concepts. The following example mixes methodological and thematic outlining. It starts with the research title in light of the specific research questions. Here is an example; let us say the title of the study is:

"Determinants of Middle-School Principal Turnover in New York City." And let us assume that the researcher came up with the following three research questions:

1. Does the school's internal working environment play a role in the principal's turnover decision?

2. Is there any relation between compensation and benefit packages of principals and their decisions to leave?

3. Are there any factors, external to the school, that contribute to principal turnover?

The following outline could help as a starting point. Outlines should not be confused as subheadings; rather, they help to organize ideas.

I. *Turnover as an Issue in School Systems*

    a. *Overview of employee turnover in school systems*

    b. *Disadvantages of turnover*

    c. *Any advantages to turnover?*

II.   *Principal Turnover*

      a.   *What do studies (national and international) say about it in a nutshell?*

      b.   *Trends (For example, a decade ago versus now...)*

III.   *Reasons for Principal Turnover*

      a.   *Internal work environment and principal turnover*

           i.   *Social environment*

           ii.   *Physical environment*

           iii.   *Resources*

      b.   *Compensation and principal turnover*

           i.   *Salary*

           ii.   *Other benefits*

      c.   *Factors external to the school as turnover reasons*

           i.   *Community involvement*

           ii.   *School location*

           iii.   *Personal situations of individuals*

      d.   *Other reasons*

IV.   *Principal Turnover in New York City*

      a.   *Compared with other metropolitan areas*

      b.   *By grade configuration (elementary, middle, and high school)*

      c.   *Measures taken by relevant body and organizations*

V.   *Theories/ Models on Studying Employee Turnover*

What to focus on? The relevant documents and publications that the researcher selected do not necessarily address all aspects of the researcher's outline. Some may touch many, while others may address one or two subheadings. Thus, the next step will be organizing the articles-and resources by the specific outline. Taking the outline above as example, one may have the following four major potential folders or as some traditionally call it "buckets": turnover as an issue in k-12 education, overview of principal turnover, reasons for principal turnover, and principal turnover in New York City.

Often times, beginning researchers are easily carried away with the information they read or collected from a certain article and tempted to use aspects of data or research that is not directly related to their work. The "buckets" will help the writer as guidelines to focus on the relevant aspects of the research literature in relation to the subject.

Which resources to use? The question of *what resources to include* provides two important perspectives to the writer, which I call *selectivity* and *objectivity*.

Selectivity: While some fields are easy to generate a long list of peer-reviewed literature from a library database, some fields are not as rich in literature. In most topics, in education and the social sciences, narrowing the list to select better resources, although a good problem to have, is a challenging job. While the general framework is "relevance," it is possible for the researcher to be inundated with an endless list of *relevant* literature. In such a situation, the researcher needs to have his or her own scale to judge which resource is more relevant to the topic than others.

The rule of thumb is screening through the lens of the following four areas: the scope/coverage of the study, the time of the study, the research methodology of the study (including the design, variables, and participants of the study), and the researcher/ publisher of the study. Each is discussed below.

Scope/coverage of the study. It is not enough the title of the literature or article matches the proposed topic. The researcher needs to see if the literature directly matches the proposed study. One way of doing this is through checking the research purpose statement. The other way is looking into the research question/s of the article.

Time of the study. Although classical studies are sometimes included, the researcher, by and large, is encouraged to look into recent articles in the topic. The researcher may start with articles published in the past five years and gradually expand further. Many topics in the social sciences could generate sufficient list of relevant articles written in the past ten years.

Research design. One way the researcher could check is through looking into the research methodology section. This section helps the researcher to decide the relevance of the article since it informs who the participants of the study were, what variables have been studied, the type of data-collection instruments used, and the type of design (qualitative, quantitative, or mixed method).

Publisher of the study. While there is no simple standard to compare peer-reviewed articles, the researcher could look into various indicators to see the quality and credibility of publishers such as the affiliations of the journals, where they are indexed, and the history of the journal (longevity). There are also institutions that rate journals based on their impact factors and categorize them by tier (if the researcher wants to go that long).

Objectivity*:* The other element to be considered, when deciding which resource to use, is the question of objectivity. The researcher should thus critically look into the study and make a concerted effort to include balanced views in the literature review document. Not all scholarly writings come from the same schools of thoughts—even those published in respected peer-reviewed journals. Reading today's education and social sciences literature, one can easily observe at least two views or schools of thoughts reflected in almost any issue.

Taking the safe schools literature as an example, you will find opposing views documented in peer-reviewed literature in which the one side argues for strong control mechanisms such as metal detectors, security cameras, and paid security officials with sniffing dogs in the schools; to the contrary, the other side argues against strong control mechanisms and suggests that educational/therapeutic approaches better serve with addressing the problem. While these are both important arguments, it is possible the researcher supports or believes in one of these views. The literature review, however, should document both views as objectively as possible; because reviewing the literature is a document of synthesis of what "the literature out there" says about the issue.

How to write a literature review? All the above preparations are fruitful only if the writer uses the sources effectively in a scholarly manner. The candidate should take into account the following as he or she writes the literature review.

a. *Have the reader in mind.* Literature review is written for an intended audience. The word selection, the argument to be made, and the message to be provided need to be appropriate and understood by the intended audience.

b. *Synthesize.* Literature review is not a fragmented collection of ideas. It should be developed and documented in a synthesized manner focusing on what the topic is all about, how and what previous studies addressed about the topic, and what is lacking in the body of research regarding the issue. In synthesizing the literature, it helps to identify any inconsistent findings, opposing predictions and contextual explanations (such as X affects Y in this context but negatively in the other). In other words, using comparative analysis of findings and contexts are some techniques for synthesizing the literature. The researcher also needs to follow a certain pattern of synthesizing the literature to be used. The commonly used method is the essay writing method where the introduction, body, and conclusion are effectively provided for each subtopic. Depending on the nature of the work to be reviewed and the type of research, the method of synthesis may differ accordingly. Fink (2010), for example, suggests five areas to be addressed in descriptive synthesis, namely, the purpose, methods, results, conclusions, and limitations.

c. *Build the Case.* Literature review is not a place to present a mere opinion or unwarranted statement. The researcher needs to logically argue and build the case for the topic under review. Thus, for any claims made, there needs to be evidence. The evidences in literature review are citations either as direct quotations or paraphrased statements. Evidences are stronger when more reliable sources are used. In the contrary, making a conclusion from a single evidence makes the argument weak and questionable. Paraphrasing gives the author the opportunity to provide multiple evidences at a time. Thus, unless absolutely necessary to quote, avoid (or minimize) direct quotation in literature review.

Final note: The literature review is a very important chapter that documents development in the area of interest. In the course of reading and analyzing about the topic, the writer not only familiarizes him- or herself about what has been studied in the area of interest but also enables to see gaps in research and be able to write a solid research proposal and a good literature review (chapter 2). A good literature review should clearly define the problem in a clear manner; summarize previous research and current works on the topic; identify relationship, contradictions, inconsistencies and gap in existing literature; and suggest the next step (APA, 2009). Table 1 provides some insight to candidates to self-evaluate and to improve the quality of their literature review.

Table 1

Meticulous versus Careless Writer

	A careful writer	A not-so-careful one
Quality of content	Sifts "gold nuggets" from piles of available resources.	Indiscriminately collects resources and often is influenced by opinion blogs, nonresearch articles, and special-interest reports.
Understanding	Reads before writing	Attempts to write before reading enough
Exhaustiveness	Includes seminal works on the topic (classic or recent development on the issue)	Overlooks seminal works and tends to write such statements as "little has been done/written in the topic."
Conceptualization	Has a clear concept map of the issue	Has no concept map on the issue. Acts like a ship without compass.
Views	Presents all relevant sides of the debate on the topic.	Carried away with a one-sided view
Feedback	Takes editorial or committee members criticism well or defends his or her work reasonably.	Either defensive or fails to address issues he or she agreed to address or both.
Expectation	Shows his or her best effort in any submissions/deliverables in content, form, and writing techniques.	Settles for the minimum expectation; and at times, depends entirely on research committee members' feedback.

Research Methodology (Chapter 3)

This chapter presents several aspects of the research methodology section of a dissertation. First, it briefly describes all about the research methods utilized. Second, it emphasizes the link between individual research and the institutions impacted by or responsible for the study. Third, it lists specific elements to be included. And finally, it explains each subsections to help the researcher better organize the chapter.

All about the Research Methods

Research methodology guides the process and how the study is conducted from beginning to the end. It is like a lesson plan to the classroom teacher, a recipe to the chef, a plan to the manager, or like a blueprint to the builder. How it is done affects the result. The good thing about a dissertation is that the candidate is the one who does both the planning (designing the methodology) and the actual implementation of the plan (conducting the research). The bad thing is that, for most candidates, a graduate dissertation is probably their first research work of such magnitude and hence they lack experience and confidence.

Cognizant of the importance of crafting appropriate research design for the overall quality of the dissertation, many graduate programs in education and the social sciences give utmost attention to the process. They commonly do two specific things. First, they offer multiple required courses in research methods. And, second, they assign a methodologist who is usually a research-methods expert on the candidate's research/dissertation committee. The reasons for doing these are to equip candidates with the needed skills and also to make sure they receive appropriate guidance and support.

Chapter 3 includes many specific details, namely, the design of the study, setting/location of the study, the procedure of selecting participants, instrumentation, data collection, reliability and validity of the study, study variables, and data-analysis techniques. These subsections are explained below with the intent of guiding the researcher on the components to be included in the chapter.

Chapter 3 starts with a recap of the study mainly by restating the purpose statement, in a paragraph or two. Then introduction of what is included in this chapter along with listing the subsections is provided in a paragraph. Then explanation of each subsection, with a separate heading for each is provided as follows.

Research Design

The research design subsection is where the type of research method to be used is explained and the specific design to be followed is stated. The research type could be quantitative, qualitative, or mixed methods.

Once the researcher has decided which type is applicable to the study and clearly argued for the decision usually supported by citation from relevant research-methods books and literature, the researcher also explains the specific design to be used in more details. If quantitative method is decided to be used, for example, further explanation is required whether it is going to be experimental or survey or correlational. These quantitative research designs are briefly explained below to help the novice researcher.

Quantitative Designs

*a. **Experimental:*** A type of research design used to explain whether an intervention influences an outcome (Creswell,2015). For example, a researcher may utilize such a design to study how *Difference in Teaching Methodology Affect Student Test Scores.* Such studies are conducted either by dividing groups into *control* and *experimental groups* or by using the same group to see the before (*pretest*) and *after (posttest)* of an intervention.

*b. **Correlational**:* A type of research design used to measure the degree of relationship between variables or whether one variable predicts the other; usually, when experimenting is not possible (Creswell, 2015, pp.338–376). A researcher who, for example, wants to study the relationship between *socioeconomic status (SES) and student achievement* may use a correlational study.

*c. **Survey***: A type of research design that describes trends in the population such as: attitudes, opinions, behaviors, characteristics of larger groups (Creswell, 2015, pp.378–424). Census is a commonly used survey study that studies the whole population. Other types of survey studies like political polls study the population through sampling a small group/miniature of the larger group/population. A researcher could use survey method, for example, to study the perception of parents of the Common Core Learning Standards.

Qualitative Designs

If a researcher plans to do qualitative method, he or she needs to explain if it is grounded theory, phenomenological, narrative, or ethnography, by citing appropriate literature and by arguing for the specific choice of analysis technique. Here is a brief description of these designs.

a. Grounded Theory: Grounded theory is applied when the intent is to generate general explanation (theory) by interviewing a single group of individuals, all of whom had experienced an action, a process, or interaction. Grounded theory can be built inductively from multiple case studies as well (Yin, 2013). The analysis usually is supported with depiction via a visual model/figure (Creswell, 2015). A researcher who, for example, wants to study school turnaround process may interview selected school administrators who successfully turned around persistently low-achieving schools and generate a theory on how to turn schools around based on their experience/practice.

b. Phenomenological Study: When the researcher is interested in describing the experiences of participants, from their perspective, as they lived it. It is an approach focused on capturing "the experiences of an activity or concept from the participant's perspective" (Gay,

Mills, & Airasian 2012, p.628). For example, a study aimed at understanding what it means to be a single-parent graduate student with young children can be studied by studying those individuals who had/have a firsthand experience as a single parent and while studying at the graduate level.

*c. **Ethnography:*** Examining or studying the shared behavior, values, and culture a group of individuals in their setting. The source of information will be multiple. Case study is a type of ethnographic research (Creswell, 2015, pp.465–501). A researcher uses ethnography, for example, to study individuals working *in a declining organization* either by spending in the organization as an employee or by spending significant amount of time in the organization.

*d. **Narrative:*** Study the lives/stories of one or more individuals or groups to document/write narrations about their experiences (Creswell, 2015). A researcher may use narration to study, for example, the experience of a *former child soldier.* Narrative studies provide a clearer picture of an experience or a story by piecing together relevant facts and experiences that otherwise are scattered and sometimes hidden in time and space.

Mixed-Methods Designs

While most studies are investigated either through quantitative or qualitative designs, there are times where a combination of both provide better result; in which case, the researcher decides to do mixed-methods research. Mixed-methods research uses a variety of approaches due to different factors. The following are the common factors that dictate the approaches.

- *Participants*: A researcher may decide to do mixed-methods study due to the nature of the research participants. This happens when the researcher wants to collect data from multiple groups and believes that one group of participant is better studied through interaction via interview and another group through survey/questionnaire to investigate the problem.

- *Nature of inquiry*. Sometimes the type of inquiry demand mixed-method study. An example of this is when the researcher wants to investigate issues that is partly answered through qualitative data and partly answered through quantitative data.

- *Strength*. A researcher may decide to conduct mixed method out of his or her belief that the research outcome will be strengthened by employing both quantitative and qualitative approach. The researcher in this case may collect data concurrently or at different times/in sequence. No particular order fits all inquiry of this nature; for example, a researcher who wants to first investigate the issue in breadth before going in-depth may start with quantitative followed by qualitative and vice versa.

Research Questions

As described in chapter 1, each research question answers aspects of the larger problem of the study. Although some institutions and dissertation committee members consider restating research questions in chapter 3 redundant, it is customary to list the research questions in this chapter.

Start this subsection by introducing the questions in a sentence or two before listing the research questions that are usually between two and five questions. While quantitative research questions take various forms, qualitative research questions are well answered with questions leading to expand understanding. Thus, questions framed in "How" are more appropriate to qualitative study.

There are several important points to remember about research questions and the way they impact the whole study. First, research questions are specific elements of the larger research topic. Second, research questions are the basis to design the data-collection instrument such as a questionnaire, interview, or observation tool. And third, the way the research questions are written impact what type of data-analysis techniques are used especially in quantitative methods. These points are briefly explained below.

a. The research questions should clearly link with the grand research topic. Let's say the researcher wants to study a topic: "Determinants of Middle-School Principal Turnover in New York City." Specific aspects of the broader topic can be explored using distinct research questions. These aspects are stated as research questions as follow:

1. Is there any relationship between the compensation and benefit package of principals and their decisions to leave?

2. Does the school internal working environment play a role in the principals' decisions to leave?

3. Are there any factors external to the schools that contribute to the principals' turnover?

b. There needs to be a clear link between the research questions and items of data-collection instrument. While instrumentation will be discussed separately in this chapter, it is noteworthy to show how items of an instrument are related to each survey research question. To answer research question 1 above (Is there any relationship between the compensation and benefit package of principals and their decisions to leave?), the researcher needs to ask several specific questions. Just inquiring about benefits alone, the researcher may ask about insurance (specifically: dental, medical, life, disability); leave (maternity, paternity, sick, paid); and other benefits (such as parking, transportation, wellness, retirement, employee assistance). For each research question, the researcher needs to make sure that sufficient and well-thought-out items are included.

c. The way research questions are written also impact the type of data-analysis techniques to be used. This will be addressed more specifically in the data-analysis section at the end of this chapter; however, it is imperative that the researcher has the data-analysis technique in mind at the early stage of the research. Looking into the same research question ("Is there any relationship between the compensation and benefit package of principals and their decisions to leave?"), the researcher is confronted with various considerations to take into account such as the following: the research design to be followed (this case for example is better studied using quantitative method); which among the long list of quantitative data-analysis techniques to choose; how the wording in the question matter (in this case "relationship" is a key word); how the nature and the type of variables to be studied (in this case, compensation/benefit and decision to leave) are appropriately investigated; the measurement scale to be used (nominal, ordinal, interval, ratio). More explanation of each of this is available in part 3.

Participants of the Study

Research participants are individuals from whom data are collected. Participants impact the outcome of the study. A careful selection of individual participants requires that the researcher understands the general population to be studied and how to conduct appropriate sampling.

Population

Population is "a large group to whom results can be generalized" (McMillan, 2012, p.96). While population refers to all in the universe in its literal meaning, in research, population can be limited to any larger group targeted for generalization. In other words, the scope/parameter of a study is what determines the population in research. For example, taking our prior example of "Determinants of Middle-School Principal Turnover in New York City," the population for this study will *not* be all principals in the world. Rather, the level and boundary of the topic narrow the population from all principals to those who share the two common characteristics of being in "middle school" and in "New York City."

Sample

Sample is defined as "a group of cases or subjects selected from the larger group in the hope that the smaller group (sample) will reveal information about the larger group (population)" (Vogt & Johnson, 2011, p.347). Ideally a sample is the *miniature* of the population it represents. However, it is not always possible to study the perfect sample/miniature that represents the population in almost all its dimensions or characteristics. Depending on the size of the population and the nature of the study, the entire population is sometimes used as a sample.

Sampling methods vary according to the purpose of the study and the nature of the population. Broadly speaking, sampling procedures follow either probability or nonprobability methods. Each of this is explained below.

Probability Sampling*:* Gives a known probability of selection/representation of all participants or subjects. There are several specific types of probability sampling.

   a. *Simple Random*: Every participant has an equal and independent chance of being selected.

Example*: Lottery or computerized selection.*

   b. *Systematic Random*: Including the "nth subject of the list in the population."

Example*: Including the subjects in every fifth number.*

   5, 10, 15, 20...

   c. *Stratified Random:* When a probability sample is taken from each category or strata. Similar to quota that is discussed below (also referred as stratified nonrandom sampling) but this one gives equal chance to each individual in the population.

Example*: Proportionately including each gender or each religious group, or each racial group to a study.*

   d. *Cluster:* A stage-by-stage sampling procedure, when there is no exhaustive list of participants. It involves multiple stages.

Example: *To study how middle-school children in New England region spend their spare time*:

   First list all the states in the New England region; then select two states randomly; then select thirty middle schools in the two states randomly and study all the students in those schools.

Nonprobability Sampling*:* Does not give a probable chance of selection or representation to all individual participants. Like probability sampling, nonprobability sampling also vary based on several factors.

Here are the most common types of nonprobability sampling techniques:

    a. *Convenience Sampling*: As the name implies, this sampling technique is based on what is easy and convenient to the researcher.

Example*: A medical doctor studying her patients.*

The rationale behind such use is this: Why identify a stranger as a participant when you already have a person with whom you built a rapport?

    b. *Snowball Sampling:* When the researcher identified some participants and asks those participants to identify or recruit others to become members of the sample. This type of sampling is particularly important in situations where sensitive issues are studied.

Example*: When a researcher wants to study a group of minors or vulnerable population who experienced certain abuse* (such as kids abused by coaches or employees forced to do unethical things by employer). The rationale behind using such sampling method is to recruit potential participants through the group members who know others that passed through the same experience.

    c. *Quota Sampling*: When the goal is to make sure representation of each distinct group is taken into account without necessarily giving equal chance to individuals in the groups.

Example*: When a researcher wants to include, for example, the voices of urban, suburban, rural residents without going any further on who should be included and in what proportion.*

Such a study is usually conducted when a quick response is needed and when resources are limited. Quota sampling is infamous for the 1948 presidential election poll where all the major polls (Gallup, Roper, and Crossley) gave the wrong prediction that Dewey would defeat Truman. This is a good example why this method is risky for large-scale inferential purposes.

    d. *Purposeful Sampling*: When the researcher makes a deliberate selection of individual participants because he or she judges they have important or relevant information for the study.

Example*: A researcher selecting "teachers of the year" for a research on effective teaching.*

Most qualitative studies fall under the Purposeful Sampling category.

Data Collection

This is the section where the researcher explains what type of data is needed for the study. Some studies require using existing data while others use collection of new data.

***Caution*!** Before approaching any human being to collect data, it is a requirement that candidates receive IRB (Institutional Review Board) approval of the proposed study. In the United States, all higher education institutions review the research proposals to make sure the rights and welfare of the research participants (human subjects) are protected and the research adheres to ethical expectations. Candidates need to work with their research advisor as early as possible to get approval from the college's IRB. Sometimes more than one IRB approval is needed if the research is conducted in multiple institutions. In most institutions, the dissertation/research advisor is considered the "principal investigator" or PI for the IRB purpose. As a signatory of your IRB application, it is in the interest of the research advisor to guide candidates through the process.

In some instances, candidates use secondary data (data already collected by others) for their research and hence have no contact with human subjects. Even in such cases, institutional IRB procedures need to be followed, as institutions vary on how they process such applications.

In the data-collection section, the researcher needs to explain what type of data is to be obtained/collected from what source in detail. The specific subsections should explain the data-collection instrument and the data-collection strategies as follow.

Instrumentation

Instrumentation, in research, refers to the type and nature of the data-collection tool such as questionnaire, interview protocol, and observation protocol. In this section, the researcher has to explain what type of instrument to be used along with the details of the instrument. This includes but is not limited to the following:

a. *Who created the instrument?* The researcher should explain if the instrument is designed by the researcher or if it is modified or adapted from another researcher's work. It is perfectly fine to use the instrument of other researchers as long as it serves the purpose of the study. However, the researcher needs to get permission from the author of the instrument, acknowledge the author appropriately, and document correspondences with the author regarding the permission. A simple copy of e-mail exchanges may serve the purpose.

b. *The subsections of the instrument:* Instruments often have multiple sections; especially when it is a questionnaire. Sections such as background information and other content-by-content subsections are customary. The researcher needs to explain the subsections in sufficient detail.

c. *The type of items or questions in the instrument.* The researcher needs to explain if the questions are open-ended, closed-ended, or mixed? If closed-ended, what type (forced choice, likert-type scale, rank order…)? In addition, the descriptions of the number and type of choices are essential. If likert-type scale is used, for example, explain how many choices are given and what each choice/scale means.

d. *How long is the instrument?* The researcher should clearly state the total number of questions in the instrument and give a reasonable estimated time needed to complete the questions.

e. *Is the instrument pilot tested?* Whether the instrument is self-designed or adapted from someone else, the researcher needs to explain the process taken to make sure the instrument is indeed a good instrument. The most common way to do this is through pilot testing, meaning, by testing the instrument in a small scale before it is used for a large-scale data gathering. Pilot testing provides feedback to the researcher, for example, on the clarity of the questions, appropriateness of the content, and even the time needed to complete the data collection. One of the criteria in choosing data-collection instruments developed by another researcher is to see if they have been pilot tested. *Part two of this book provides detailed guide(with samples) on how to design data collection instruments.*

Data-Collection Strategies

The researcher is expected to clearly state how data are collected from beginning to the end. These steps include:

a. *How initial contact is made and in what way*? The researcher needs to explain the process followed to contact individuals or organizations for data-collection purpose. This includes if permission is needed and who granted that permission. For example, the collection of data from vulnerable population or minors needs to follow the proper informed consent and/or assent process based on the approved IRB.

b. *The manner in which data is collected.* This varies by the nature of the study. If it is quantitative study, for example, was the data collected via online instrument or using paper and pencil? If it is collected via online survey, how is the link sent to respondents? If paper and pencil, who administered the instrument? Was it mailed? For qualitative study, this includes whether the interview is recorded or not, and how? Where is the interview conducted? Is it face-to-face? And the like.

c. *What is done to maximize response*? Explain the process followed to maximize response including but not limited to follow-up process, the time window for data collection, and if any remuneration is used as per the IRB application.

Reliability and Validity

A standard scientific study such as a master's thesis and doctoral dissertation should document reliability and validity in sufficient detail.

Reliability

Research should be free from measurement error. One way to safeguarding the research from such errors is through the assurance of "consistency" or "stability" of the measure when repeated. Here is an example: Let's say a trooper administers a breathalyzer test on a suspected drunk driver. The machine shows 0.145 the first time. The officer tried it on the same person after a few seconds and recorded a 0.05. Puzzled by the difference, the officer tested the suspect for the third time in a few minutes and the machine showed 0.08. The question is, is this machine *reliable*? Is it believable? And the answer is NO! The same is true when a researcher talks about reliability. A research instrument should give consistent results if repeated in the same manner and similar context.

So, before starting data collection and analysis of findings, the researcher should clearly guard the process from measurement error. This is the section where this process is clearly described. The researcher may use and explain one or more of the following techniques to assure consistency/reliability.

a. *Inter-rater reliability:* Consistency between two or more raters in their observation or measuring of the same phenomenon. For example, two individuals used the same observation checklist to observe a teacher in a classroom (same teacher, same classroom, and same time). Comparing the two ratings, the researcher can judge if the results are consistent or not.

b. *Test-retest reliability:* Stability or variability of the same measure or instrument when used at different times.

c. *Parallel-form reliability:* Stability of result when different versions of the same test/questionnaire are administered. For example, a teacher has an item bank of twenty questions that assess the same content, are constructed in the same way, and test the same knowledge base. She decides to split this into two tests (test 1 and test 2), each with ten items, and administers test 1 for half of her students and test 2 for the rest. The two tests are reliable if produced similar results.

d. *Internal consistency reliability:* The consistency of items in an instrument that measure the same construct. Cronbach's alpha is a widely used test for internal consistency in quantitative study. Example, a researcher has a questionnaire of twenty items that probe whether participants are happy in their work place. What Cronbach's alpha measures is whether the twenty items are really consistent in measuring the construct "workplace happiness."

Note: It is *not* enough that the research instrument is reliable. For example, if the breathalyzer machine consistently recorded 0.05 in all the three tests, in the prior example, there is still a need for validation to check the accuracy. Consistency doesn't guarantee accuracy! A liar could lie consistently! That doesn't make the story true! That is why we need another measure to make sure the results are accurate—which is *validity*!

Validity

Scientific research needs to be both reliable and valid. An instrument or a test is valid if it measures what it is supposed to measure. Validity of an instrument answers the question, "Can we obtain accurate result through the said instrument?" For example, a test used to screen applicants for college admissions is valid if its scores are directly related to the candidates' future college academic performance.

There are several types of validity.

a. *Construct Validity*: Is a type of validity test on whether a construct measures the concept/phenomenon it is supposed to measure. For example, if a researcher wants to study mastery of a certain *skill* (which is the construct) through a set of questions; do those questions really measure the said skill?

b. *Content Validity*: This is a type validity focused at measuring whether the tool/instrument fully covers the content to be measured.

c. *Face Validity* is a type of content validity where a quick scan of an instrument is done for its face value, for example, by someone who has a subject-matter expertise on the content.

d. *Criterion Validity*: A type of validity that shows the effectiveness of an instrument to predict future achievement. For example, if a third-grade math test result on a teacher designed test predicts or concurs the result of the statewide third-grade test result, the teacher designed test is considered valid.

Reliability and Validity in Qualitative Research

Qualitative researchers need to explain how reliability and validity is achieved both in the collection and analysis of data. Here are some common ways to do so (Merriam 2001 ; Creswell 2014):

a. *Triangulation:* Using multiple data source or multiple mechanism of data collection is one way of documenting the reliability and internal validity of qualitative study. The researcher, therefore, needs to articulate how triangulation is done by providing multiple evidence on the accuracy of data (validity) from multiple sources to check its consistency (reliability).

b. *Thick Description:* One way of ensuring the validity of qualitative study is through thick and rich description of data throughout the presentation and analysis of data. The researcher may explain validity, for example, by detailing the situation in which data is collected, explaining the relevance of the data source, and also by ensuring the use of the research participants' words via direct quotation or rich description.

c. *Member Checking:* The researcher benefits from feedback on the way he or she used the data throughout the analysis. A commonly used approach in qualitative study is to invite research participants to provide feedback on the accurate representation (validity) of the data they provided, before the study is completed.

d. *Peer Examination/Debriefing:* The researcher also benefits from the feedback on data presentation and interpretation from colleagues or individuals who share the views of the study participants, before the study is completed. The researcher should explain how the peer examination is conducted to ensure validity of the study.

e. *Researcher Bias/Position:* Like anybody else, a researcher may have a position or view on the issue to be studied. The researcher, however, should make sure his or her view doesn't affect the interpretation and the outcome of the study. The researcher may do, and document, the following to mitigate bias and ensure reliability: inform the readers about his or her position and view that were brought to the study, personal reflection on the position held in view of the data collected, and reading and rereading the transcript to base the analysis and interpretation on the data rather than prior views.

Threats to External Validity

External validity differs in meaning and approach between quantitative and qualitative designs. For quantitative research, it is about *generalizability* while for qualitative research, it is about *transferability*. Research results need to be guarded from threats to external validity.

Generalizability is affected by the nature of participants, the location/setting of the study, the treatment, and the time when study is conducted (McMillan,2012 and Trochim, 2006). To minimize threat that lead to wrong generalization: (a) the participants/sample should be typical of the population targeted for generalization; (b) the location/setting of the study should not be unusual; (c) the study should withstand slight variation in treatment; and (d) the timing of the research shouldn't have unusual positive or negative influence on the study.

External validity in qualitative research is about the transferability of research results to other similar situations with similar characteristics in terms of context and parameters used (Lincoln & Guba, 1986). Threats to transferability of a qualitative study are minimized by providing detailed context/setting of the study and sufficiently describing the assumptions of the study or the environment /situation surrounding the research. Although it is up to the readers or users to decide whether or not the research is applicable to transfer to the intended purpose, the researcher has a responsibility to provide sufficient background to help readers make informed decision.

Study Variables

The researcher is expected to describe the study variables in this section. A variable is any factor or entity that changes in values. Trochim (2006, n.p.) underlines the importance of understanding study variables when he states that "you won't be able to do very much in research unless you know how to talk about variables." This is very true as the essence of research is all about explaining variance or variability.

So the researcher needs to explain the *study variables* as clearly as possible. Study variables are those variables mentioned in the research questions/hypothesis or in the purpose statement of your study. Variables could be either quantitative or qualitative. Quantitative variables are those that change in magnitude or number where as qualitative variables are those that change in attribute or characteristics (Wang, 2004).

The common expectation in writing this section of the dissertation of a quantitative study is to describe the independent and dependent variables. Independent variables are those variables whose change affects the outcome of other variables under study (dependent variables). Dependent variables are those being affected by the change in the independent variables.

Consider our prior example of the following research question: "How does school climate contribute to middle-school principals' turnover?" The independent variable here is school climate, while the dependent variable is principal turnover. For each research question or hypothesis, the researcher is expected to explain these variables.

Data-Analysis Techniques

Data-analysis techniques are specific procedures followed to make sense or meaningful explanation of the collected raw data. In chapter 4, the researcher will be presenting the data analyses. Here, the researcher tells readers what procedure to be followed and lays the foundation for what will be done in the next chapter.

The first three chapters of your dissertation are also called the research proposal. By design, proposals talk about the future: what and how to accomplish. This subsection of chapter 3 is crucial and highly scrutinized before the proposal is approved, since it links the proposal to the action.Data-analysis techniques vary by the nature of data collected and the type of inquiry. Quantitative analysis of data, for example, follows a different approach than qualitative analysis.

Quantitative Data-Analysis Techniques. If the proposed study is quantitative, the researcher needs to clearly explain the statistical techniques that will be used to answer each research question or to test the hypotheses. As explained in section 3.1, the researcher has already decided what type of quantitative research design to use for the study earlier. In this section, what the researcher is required is to more specifically describe the statistical-analysis technique for answering each research question.

Depending on the nature of the study, the researcher may use multiple statistical techniques throughout the dissertation. The decision of these techniques is based on several factors but the following two are crucial:

a. *Clarity on what the research question intends to examine*: Is it relationships? Difference? Impact? Predictions? Descriptions? etc.

b. *Understanding the nature of the variables to be examined*: How many dependent and independent variables are there? What is the nature of the distribution of scores? What are the levels of measurement of each variable (ordinal, nominal, ratio, or interval)? And how are the relevant questions of the survey/questionnaire framed? Answering these questions will help in deciding specific statistical techniques.

Many quantitative research-methods books present a statistical decision-making chart or tool to help beginning researchers in the selection of specific data-analysis techniques. See Appendix A: Statistical Decision Tree.

Qualitative Data-Analysis Techniques. Qualitative researchers need to thoroughly document the process of organizing and presenting data. Qualitative data is collected through interview, observation, and document review and artifacts collection. These raw data have to be organized, coded, and categorized into themes. In the case of interviews, the audio/video data need to be transcribed before doing all these steps. In this section, the researcher should tell the readers, step by step, the process he or she will be following in converting the raw data into a meaningful analysis. The researcher may ask the following questions to help write a good data-analysis strategy:

- What type of data am I using (interview, observation, document review, artifacts)?
- Who transcribes the interview? (self, bond transcriptionist, using software?)
- How many times should I read the transcription to understand the data?
- Should I start organizing the data while the data collection is ongoing or after it is completed? (Either is fine.)
- What type of coding should I use?
- Should I expect the themes to emerge from the data or should I expect the themes beforehand, based on my familiarity with the literature on the topic?

After the researcher answered these questions, the next step will be putting them in writing, in a logical sequence or preferred style. See Appendix B: Qualitative Data Analysis Process.

Data-Analysis Software. Another important point to mention in the data-analysis subsection of a dissertation is the software to be used to analyze the data. The researcher needs to have a good understanding of the relevance of the software for the specific study before picking one. Quantitative researchers often use statistical software programs such as SPSS (that is most commonly used in dissertations and theses), STATA, SAS, EXCEL, and so forth. Qualitative researchers use such data-analysis software as NVivo, MAXQDA, ATLAS.ti, Hyper Research, Dedoos, and so forth. Mixed-methods researchers may use a combination of qualitative and quantitative software for each type of data.

Software, like any technology, has its own pros and cons regarding when we use it and what we use itfor, due to the amount of investment it needs and the learning curve it requires. The rule of thumb in using qualitative data-analysis software, according to Gay, Mills, and Airasian (2009, p.455), was to use qualitative software if you affirmatively answered the following:

- Your data is large (more than five hundred pages)
- You can be adequately trained to use the software?
- You have the resources to purchase?
- You need to be able to capture specific quotes from a large database?

However, as technology is rapidly changing, it is possible that software prices and ease of use will not continue to be challenges, thereby attracting more and more candidates to use qualitative software for data analysis even when the transcriptions are not bulky.

Final Note: Writing the research methodology chapter requires a strong foundation and a thorough understanding of the type of research method in general and the data analysis techniques to be followed in specific. I found the following resources to be useful to my students in the past:

1. **Qualitative Research Resources:**

    Merriam, S.B. (2009). *Qualitative Research: A Guide to Design and Implementation*. San Francisco, CA: Jossey-Bass.

    Yin, R. K. (2015). Qualitative research from start to finish. New York, NY: Guilford Publications.

2. **Quantitative Research Resources:**

    Field, A. (2009). *Discovering statistics using SPSS*. Thousand Oaks, CA: Sage publications.

    Salkind, N. J. (2015). *Statistics for people who (think they) hate statistics* Thousand Oaks, CA: Sage publications

3. **General Research Resources (including mixed Methods)**

    Creswell, J. W. (2013). *Research design: Qualitative, quantitative, and mixed methods approaches*. Thousand Oaks, CA: Sage publications.

    McMillan, J. H. (2012). *Educational research: Fundamentals for the consumer*. Boston, MA: Pearson

    Vogt, W.P., Gardner, D.C. & Haefelle, L.M. (2012). *When to use what research design*. New York, NY: The Guilford Press.

Data Analysis (Chapter 4)

Data analysis is a process of finding answers to the research questions based on data. Once the required data is collected following the procedure outlined in the research proposal, the researcher is confronted with the raw data that needs to be organized and manipulated to look for meanings as he or she answers the research questions. After the data is organized and meaningful outputs are discovered, the researcher presents the results supported by concrete evidences from the data.

In a standard five-chapter dissertation, the fourth chapter is where data analysis is presented. Elements of chapter 4 include an opening paragraph on the purpose of the chapter followed by a brief description of the study, background information of research participant, the findings of the study, and summary of the chapter. Before discussing the specific elements of the dissertation, let us see what the process of data analysis looks like in general.

The Process of Data Analysis

Understanding the process of data analysis is very important for any researcher, especially for the novice ones, before jumping into the writing phase.

Answering the following questions, I believe, helps to give us a vivid picture of the process. What is data analysis anyway? When is it appropriate to begin data analysis? Who should be involved in analyzing the data? What is the role of technology to analyze the data? What is the role of the researcher in meaning making?

Data analysis defined. "Data analysis" is the process of making sense or meaning out of the raw data or information collected or obtained by the researcher. Data comes in many forms, and it is collected using various forms of instruments. We collect data through questionnaires and interviews. We also collect data through observation, document review, and accessing various artifacts such as pictures, videos, physical sites, and materials. Data analysis involves understanding the data, mining relevant information from the vast data set collected for the research, and answering the specific research question posed using the data as evidence by employing appropriate data-analysis techniques. In sum, "one analyzes data so as to be able to interpret them, to make sense of them, to figure out what they tell—if anything" (Vogt, 2007, p.15).

When to begin data analysis. Data analysis generally begins after data collection is completed. In qualitative research, however, researchers sometimes prefer to code and categorize data while data collection is in progress. This process of organizing qualitative data should not be confused with data analysis.

Once the researcher has completed collecting the needed data, the raw data has to be prepared for analysis. This is done by carefully inspecting the data for its cleanliness and completeness. Data inspection involves editing the collected data as needed.

Raw data could have many possible errors, which potentially harms the analysis process and may damage the output of the research if left without careful inspection. The researcher has to double-check suspicious figures and missing values. Such errors are very common especially when dealing with quantitative data.

The sources of such errors could either be the specific research participant or the researcher. Some errors are fixable, while others are difficult to fix after the fact. The researcher has to check the source of the error before either attempting to fix or proceeding to analyze the data. The first step in the process of error checking is to go back and look into individual responses from the completed questionnaires, whether paper and pencil or electronic.

There are usually two possibilities for such errors. The first possibility is that perhaps the participant carelessly (or inadvertently) provided a wrong response. The second possibility is that the participant correctly wrote the response, but the data was recorded wrong due to data-entry error.

Once the researcher knows where the problem is, the next step will be to determine if the error is fixable or not. In the examples above, errors made by the participants are not fixable, as the researcher cannot go back and ask the participants about their responses for various reasons. (It is even impossible to know who answered what in the case of anonymous studies). Thus, such data need to be excluded or treated as a missing data. Data-entry errors, on the other hand, are usually fixable, since the error is made by the researcher during data entry (this often happens when manually entering data). The researcher may simply substitute the wrong figure with the correct response from the questionnaire and use the cleaned data for analysis.

While the above example is based on quantitative data collection, it is important that the researcher inspects any form of data, including qualitative ones. The researcher needs to make sure the record and data match with the respective participant. Steve's response, for example, should not be presented as John's. Writing the names or pseudonyms of respondents on each page of the interview transcript and observation note is a prudent way of keeping the data from a possible error (data contamination) resulting from misplacement. Similarly, what is usually called "member checking" is another important process of guarding qualitative data from erroneous data reporting. Although member checking as a validity measure happens after the first draft of the data analysis is completed, it is a very good way of data cleaning before the research goes public.

In addition to inspecting the raw data, the researcher needs to check if coding is done correctly. A simple coding error may cause a big problem. Imagine a researcher who coded Male as 1 and Female as 2 but entered in the database otherwise, thereby reporting completely opposite results in the data analysis. This could be catastrophic!

A careful scrutiny is required from any researcher to minimize errors that emerge from such defective data. Thus, it is incumbent on the researcher to have clean and complete data before starting the data analysis.

Who should be involved in analyzing the data? Writing a dissertation, in general, is the individual candidate's responsibility. The whole idea of why higher education institutions include dissertation completion as a requirement or partial requirement, in their curriculum, is to prepare graduates with the skills of independently conducting and using research. It is, therefore, an independent work. This doesn't mean, however, that the candidate is left alone in the dark. For almost everybody passing through doctoral program, writing a dissertation is a first-time experience, except for those few overachievers aspiring multiple doctorates. Cognizant of this, colleges and universities offer multiple research-methods courses and assign faculty as dissertation committee members to help candidates successfully navigate through the research process.

Candidates may seek technical help in other aspects of the dissertation process, such as data collection, transcription of qualitative data, data entry, running data-analysis software, and editing. However, when it comes to data analysis, including decisions on the type of data-analysis techniques to be used, interpreting the result, and writing the report are the sole responsibilities of the candidate.

The role of technology to analyze data. We live in the age of technological advancement! Thank God! Like in any other aspect of our lives, technology has made research work handy. Back in the day, researchers had to travel from place to place to collect data before it was replaced by the technology of postal services and now the Internet. We now collect quantitative data via electronic survey, use software that enter data directly to our electronic database while data collection is in progress, and run software to analyze electronic data set to get research output in our finger tips. Similarly, qualitative researchers now use various types of technologies to collect, record, transcribe, and code data. A list of data-analysis software can be found in the "Data-Analysis Techniques" section of chapter 3.

While technology is expected to advance even at a faster pace in the future, it takes a researcher to craft or adapt quality data-collection instruments such as questionnaires and interviews, design appropriate research methodology, choose the right data-analysis technique, and "command" the respective software to generate the needed output.

In short, it should be noted that the application of technology in doctoral research is to optimize the research process; it is not to substitute or replace the researcher's role altogether. The thinking, analyzing, and writing the report are still the researcher's role!

The role of the researcher in meaning making. Data analysis goes beyond presenting data or information. The researcher needs to provide meaning to the data and information not only in the global context of the purpose of the research but also in relation to each research question or hypothesis. If a data segment has no meaning or relevance to the intended research, it should not be presented in the research document.

Data presentation takes many forms. In quantitative research numerical data may be presented, for example, in the form of tables, figures, diagrams, charts, and graphs. Examples of qualitative-research data presentation, on the other hand, may include quotations (direct and paraphrased) from interviews, observation notes, pictures, and citations of relevant documents. Meaning making entails supporting the claims or statements with evidence. In so doing, the researcher presents the data and interprets them to the level of the intended reader.

For the quantitative researcher, it is not enough to present data in organized manner, such as tables, charts, figures, graphs; the researcher needs to explain them as well. The explanation takes different forms, from description to interpreting specific figures with specific emphasis to explaining the level of significance of statistical tests and outputs, depending on the type of the statistical-analysis techniques used. Similarly, the qualitative researcher's job of data analysis goes beyond presenting themes that emerge from the data through citing and paraphrasing quotations or documenting artifacts. The researcher needs to explain how the presented data answers the intended research inquiry in unambiguous manner.

Components of Chapter 4

Elements/components of chapter 4 commonly include an opening paragraph on the purpose of the chapter followed by a brief description of the study, background information of the participants along with the rate of return, the findings of the study, and summary of the chapter. Each element is discussed below.

Purpose of the chapter. From the beginning the researcher needs to explain the purpose of the chapter. He or she may simply describe what is to be included in the chapter and list the contents in the order they appear. This should not be unnecessarily long. A paragraph or two may suffice.

Brief description of the purpose of the study. After explaining the purpose of chapter, the next logical step will be providing a brief description of the purpose of the research in general. This too should be brief. A summarized description in a page or two should be enough. All in all, this includes what the research is about, where the study was conducted (the location), who the targeted population were, and what research design or tradition was followed.

Background of participants. The "Background of Participants" section is often a stand-alone subheading in chapter 4 of a standard dissertation. This is the section where the researcher explains to the reader who the research participants were. This includes the total invited participants and those who took part in the study. In quantitative study, stating the rate of return both in number and percentage is essential. In general, this section describes the nature of participants in terms of the demographic characteristics the researcher collected, such as gender, level of education, work experience, and so forth. Usually this is presented in a table followed by a brief description. In qualitative research, an in-depth or rich description of the setting of the research along with the individual participants of the study is very important. This helps the reader to understand how the proposed data-collection strategy, mentioned in chapter 3, went as planned.

Helpful information in this regard includes where the interviews or observations were conducted, how long it took, what happened during the interviews or observations that affected the study, who the interviewees were, and when data collection was completed. When describing the background of individual participants, the researcher needs to make sure that the identities of human subjects are protected as per the approved IRB protocol for the study.

Presentation and analyses of data. While approaches of presenting the data vary according to the research methodology used, preferences of the dissertation committee members, and specific institutional guidelines/requirements, the following specific elements help to guide the presentation and analysis of data in general.

Data presentation needs to follow a certain structure of analysis. In quantitative research, the most widely used model of data analysis is a question-by-question structure. The researcher states the first research question and then presents the data and analyzes the respective outcome before addressing the next research question. The same structure is sometimes used in a qualitative approach with multiple research questions. However, a qualitative researcher may better organize the structure of the analysis by meaningful segments or themes in a logical flow to provide meaningful narratives through connecting aspects of data to address the inquiry in totality.

The researcher, at this point, has already decided the type of analysis/statistical technique to be used for each research question. Thus, before presenting the data or outputs, the researcher needs to explain to the reader the specific analysis technique after introducing the research question. This is particularly important for quantitative research, since each research question could require a different statistical-analysis technique. A research question that investigates relationship between variables, for example, employs a different technique than that which examines differences between variables. In qualitative study, a single analysis technique, such as narrative, ethnographic, phenomenological, or grounded theory, guides the entire study, even when multiple research questions are used. It is not enough just to state "the study is quantitative" or "qualitative" or "mixed"; the specific data-analysis technique along with the rationale for using it should be explained before presenting the data and describing the output.

The other very important element that needs to be restated before presenting data is the study variables. While stating the dependent and independent variables may not be appropriate for some descriptive quantitative studies and qualitative studies, a general description of what is being studied helps the reader to connect the data-analysis technique with the output being presented.

After the researcher has stated the research question, explained the data-analysis techniques, and restated the study variables, the next logical step is to present the data. Data presentation for quantitative study must show aggregate numbers or figures consistent with the output sought and the data-analysis techniques used. Most commonly, quantitative data is presented in a table followed by a summary or description of the finding using appropriate research language. Depending on the nature of the study, the researcher may also present using graphs and charts.

Qualitative analysis mostly uses words (as opposed to numbers) such as interview transcription and observation notes as data. Other data sources for qualitative data include but are not limited to photos, videos, audios, and archival data. The researcher needs to provide rich evidence from such data to support any claims or statements reached by way of data analysis. Qualitative data analysis is effectively organized around the themes that emerged from the data. While the codes that are extracted from the raw data (such as interview transcripts) lead to the development of themes, the researcher needs to make a strong case under each theme through providing direct quotations, paraphrases, and other concrete evidence relevant to the stated theme.

In the process of presenting the findings, the researcher is expected to explain what they mean. This includes interpreting of the findings, providing meaning, and providing rationale why the specific finding is important. For example, a quantitative researcher may present a correlation table to show the relationship between variables of the study. The researcher is expected to indicate: which results are significant, the strength of the significance, the direction of the relationship, what the relationship tells.

Example

The following correlation table may help to test several hypotheses, but for our purpose, let's assume the researcher wanted to test relationships between organizational productivity and the following five organizational factors: employee motivation, employee experience, employee creativity, employee turnover, and leadership stability.

Table 2.

Correlation between organizational productivity and five organizational factors.

Measure	1	2	3	4	5	6
1. Employee motivation	—					
2. Employee experience	.52**	—				
3. Employee creativity	.70**	.74**	—			
4. Employee turnover	-.41**	-.72**	-.21	—		
5. Leadership stability	.14	.11	.33	-.67**	—	
6. Organizational productivity	.40**	.25	.80*	-.66*	.61*	—

P < .01*, p < .05**

The analysis for the data presented in table two above may look like the following.

As presented in Table 2 above, relationships exist between organizational productivity and four of the variables in the study (employee salary, employee creativity, employee motivation, and leadership stability). However, the strength and direction of relationships vary.

Employee Creativity has a statistically significant and a very strong positive correlation (r = .80, p < .01) with organizational productivity. Similarly, a significant positive strong relationship exists between leadership stability and organizational productivity (r = .61, p < .01). A moderate, but significant relationship also exists between employee motivation and organizational productivity (r = .40, p < .05). On the other hand, employee turnover and organizational productivity have a significant, strong inverse relationship (r = -.66, p < .01). No significant relationship was found between employee experience and organizational productivity. The correlation analysis results tell us that high level of organizational productivity is associated with high level of employee creativity, high level of leadership stability, high employee motivation, and low level of employee turnover.

Bottom-line: The objective of data analysis is to answer research questions the researcher raised. Effective data analysis ends with providing answer to the stated question/hypothesis. The findings may or may not agree or corroborate with previous researches of the same kind or the researcher's expectations. The researcher should not be influenced by such background noises. He or she is expected to base the analysis on the data and the data alone.

Final Note: Depending of the institutional format for dissertation or the preference of your dissertation committee, you may be asked to analyze your findings in view of previous research. This author used a format where such analyses is done in the conclusions subsection of chapter five.

Summary of Findings, Conclusions, and Recommendations (Chapter 5)

The standard five-chapter dissertation ends with a chapter that summarizes the research findings, provides conclusions, and suggests recommendations. Often, readers who don't have time to go through the entire dissertation, focus on this chapter to get information about the process and outcome of the study. It is a kind of a one-stop shopping for the quick reader. Thus, the researcher needs to pay due attention in writing and organizing this chapter.

Writing chapter 5 is both simple and challenging. It is simple because it is written after the researcher has written the first four chapters, which provide what is needed to write the chapter. This means that most of the information presented in chapter 5 is in one way or another presented in the previous chapters. In addition, in the process of writing the four chapters, the researcher has gained wider perspectives on the topic and elevated self to the status of expert on the matter.

On the other hand, it is challenging, because it requires the researcher to think thoroughly, to provide conclusive statements, and to suggest expert advice; all of which demand the ability of writing to the point in a concise and clear manner. While the writer is usually judged by the entire work, often, readers form their opinions about the research and the researcher based on what they see in chapter 5.

In sum, the way this chapter is organized and presented is crucial. The components of chapter 5 along with specific outlines on what to include and not to include in the chapter is presented below.

Components of Chapter 5

This chapter starts with a transition that briefly describes the study in general terms, in a page or two. Important to include in this section are a brief recap of what is studied, what necessitated the study, how the study was conducted, and who the participants of the study were.

Once an appropriate transition is made, the researcher lists the subcomponents of the chapter in the order they are presented. The most commonly used subcomponents or subsections include *Summary of Findings, Conclusions, and Recommendations.* Some formats include *Implications and Recommendation for Further Studies.*

What are these subcomponents all about? What information needs to be included under each subcomponent? How do these subcomponents differ and relate to each other? These questions are addressed below while addressing each subcomponent.

Summary of Findings

The first subcomponent of chapter 5 is "Summary of Findings." As the name suggests, this subsection summarizes the findings of the study that were presented in chapter 4. In short, summary of findings is the "reader's digest" version of chapter 4. The major difference between chapter 4 and the summary of findings section of chapter 5 is in the level of detail included. While chapter 4 includes details about the data-analysis techniques used, the nature of variables, the nature of participants followed by a detailed data presentation with graphic and numeric display and interpretation of results, the summary of findings focuses on what is studied and what the research found. In other words, while chapter 4 documents the process and the result along with the evidence, the summary of findings highlights the result in a summarized fashion.

Although formats of writing the summary of findings subsection differ from college to college, the subsection should provide a clearly articulated summary that addresses each research question. The finding for each research question should either be presented in separate paragraphs or through restating the research questions one by one. Each finding should neither be ambiguous nor hidden. It should stand on its own.

Some common mistakes that researchers make when writing this subsection include the use of literature, quotes, and presentations of tables. While literature citations in relation to the findings may be appropriate later in the chapter in the conclusions subsection, it should be avoided in this subsection since this section is meant to clearly present your findings—what you found. In addition, since relevant tables are presented in chapter 4, the researcher may reference those tables, if there is a need, rather than being redundant.

Conclusions

The next subsection in a commonly used five-chapter dissertation is "Conclusions." After stating the findings, the researcher is expected to support them with conclusive statements. These statements tell what the findings mean in relation to what is already known about the topic. They also provide a new perspective to look at the topic. The researcher has to make a convincing case to the readers through thoughtful ideas, well-written arguments, and a complete view of the topic. While some dissertation formats differ in how this subsection should be written, writing at least one conclusion per finding makes more sense. Thus, make sure that for each finding you provided in the previous section ("Summary of Findings"), you have a corresponding conclusion in this section.

Basic Characteristics of Good Conclusions

i. *Conclusions are drawn from the research.* The researcher should be careful not to go outside the boundary of the research. Often, novice researchers drift from the study by allowing their opinion, bias or prior knowledge dominate the tone of the conclusion, inadvertently relegating the outcome of the research.

ii. *Conclusions should focus on the main points ("nuggets") of the study.* Writing a dissertation requires various skills, one of such skills is *"sifting the grain from the chaff."* Although the entire dissertation is valuable for the researcher, when it comes to writing the conclusions, the researcher has to choose a few, of high importance, statements to make the conclusions needed to represent the study as a whole.

iii.   *Conclusions show the outcome of the study in comparison to other/similar studies.* The researcher conducts the study with a purpose, guided by certain points of references. The references could be models previously developed or studies conducted in the past. Often, the researcher documents such references in the previous chapters (usually in literature review/chapter 2). When writing the conclusions of the study, the researcher needs to revisit the literature and cite appropriately as he or she compares and contrasts the research outcome vis-à-vis previous studies.

iv.   *Conclusions provide implications for the field of study.* Research has to have some kind of implication for the field of study the research addresses. These implications include providing a solution to a problem, challenging the status quo, improving practice, proposing new ways of doing things, or providing directions and frameworks for policy and research. Effective conclusions address the effect of the particular study to the broader field of study with one or more of such implications in mind.

Some institutions' dissertation formats put "Implications" as a stand-alone subcomponent of chapter 5 in addition to the three subcomponents (Summary of Findings, Conclusions, and Recommendations). Other institutions replace it for Recommendations. In any case, its importance is unquestionable.

v.   *Conclusions should be meticulously written.* It is assumed that the conclusions are statements that represent the researcher's best thinking. The researcher, therefore, should exert utmost effort that the conclusions reflect his or her mastery of the research and relevant developments surrounding the topic of the study. The researcher has to write to the level of the audience (in this case, other scholars, with graduate-level background). This means, the statements should be written carefully, well argued, unbiased, informative, and free of careless technical/grammatical errors.

Recommendations

Recommendations are by and large considered as "expert advice," the researcher being the expert now. At this point of the dissertation journey, the researcher shifts gear to look at his or her study in a global perspective. This subsection is subtly related to the "significance of the study" subsection of chapter 1. There, the researcher has listed how the study will benefit practitioners, policy makers, and researchers.

In this subsection, the researcher needs to list his or her suggestions in a clear manner having in mind practitioners, policy makers, and researchers.

Basic Characteristics of Recommendations

Generally speaking, recommendations:

i.   *Are stated in "Should" Statements.* "Should" statements suggest that the person offering the recommendation has done his or her job in due diligence and has the authority to provide such statements. As a person who conducted original research dissertation, the researcher has now the responsibility of providing advice with a tone of an expert. One way of doing that is through framing his or her sentence in a "Should" statement.

ii.   *Should not be mere common knowledge.* In this day and age, it looks like everybody has an opinion on almost every topic. Some of the opinions are often pretty generic and voicing them don't require conducting research. If your study is about drunk driving, for example, please don't write a recommendation that looks like "Drivers should not drive if they are drunk."

iii.   *Should be practical as opposed to rhetorical:* Often times graduate studies focus on philosophical issues and debates or arguments that may not necessarily have to be applied. However, what is to be recommended should be something that can be practically applied. Using the same example of the drunk-driver research, please don't recommend that "All drivers should totally avoid driving on route X because the drunk drivers love that road." That is not practical! Think something else!

iv.   *Should be based on the research.* What makes research different from opinion is that the former is scientifically designed and uses data. The researcher, although speaking in "should" statements in this subsection, doesn't have the liberty to recommend his or her opinion. Recommendations should be well-thought out and written taking into account such elements as the following:

- o the findings of the research
- o the policy/legal framework that governs the issue
- o the current technology
- o best practices
- o cultural context
- o the capacity of organizations to whom the recommendation is directed.

Using our prior example of "drunk driving," please don't recommend that "People with driver's licenses should not drink at all" or "Car manufacturers should invent cars with a drunk-driving mode that drive safely," as these are not practical, at least at the moment, and are beyond the purview of an academic researcher.

Recommendations for Further Study

In the course of exploring the topic and studying the subject, the researcher may realize that more research is needed to fully understand or better investigate the issue. The researcher then lists what he or she believes needed to be studied and presents it in this subsection. The initial list at times gets unreasonably long. The researcher needs to have a strategy to narrow them. The following elements help to frame your recommendations for further study:

i. *Magnitude:* How broad or in-depth has the problem been studied in the past? This is where you examine the body of research about the issue, including your study, to see if the topic has been studied in a small scale or wider context. If it has not been studied in a wider scale and you have a reason to recommend, then those recommendations related to breadth will be good candidates from your long list. On the other hand, if you realize that the problem has not been studied in-depth and you think a deeper look at the issue may be necessary, then you will recommend accordingly.

ii.   *Location:* The other way to look at the problem is in terms of geographical location. If all the studies about the problem, for example, have been studied in an urban context and you are curious if the result will be different in rural or suburban settings, a recommendation addressing this can be included in your list.

iii.   *Time*: How often has the issue been studied? If you think continuous study is needed (be it longitudinal or cross-sectional) to fully or better understand the issue, and you have a good reason about it, then such recommendations are reasonable.

iv.   *Design*: Has the topic been studied using different research methodologies? If the topic, for example, was never or little examined using qualitative method and you have a good reason to recommend a qualitative study that can be a good reason.

v.   *Participants:* Sometimes the researcher may believe that studying the issue using other groups of individuals will yield important results. If the body of research predominantly focused on small children and the researcher has a good reason to recommend a study in adults or seniors, that can be another candidate for the list of recommendation.

Final Note: When writing chapter 5, the candidate should always bear in mind the connection of the findings with the conclusions and recommendations. Although the findings, conclusions, and recommendations are relatively written in a more elaborated way, the following fictitious example shows the connection, in a simplistic manner.

Finding 1: This study revealed that women constitute 40 percent of all principals and 18 percent of all superintendents nationwide, out of which 70 percent of principals and 84 percent of superintendents will be eligible to retire in the next five years.

Conclusion 1: Women administrators both at building and system levels remain underrepresented. Compared to a similar nationwide study conducted over a decade ago (Morgan 2003), there is only a slight increment in the percentages of both women principals and superintendents, which, respectively, were 38 percent and 17 percent. The current trend is even alarming given the overwhelming majority of women school administrators are approaching their retirement.

Recommendations 1: Female educators in K–12 schools nationally outnumber their male counterparts. However, administrative positions are disproportionately held by male educators. This problem points to a possible lack of access of administrative positions to women educators. School districts **should** evaluate their administrator hiring, promotion, and retention process to improve the underrepresentation of women administrators at building and district levels.

Part 2: Data-Collection Instruments

The Need for Data-Collection Instruments

We cannot talk about research without data. We cannot also conduct research using any data. What makes research different from opinion or simple journalistic reporting is that research is based on relevant, sufficient, and accurate information, which are attributes of quality data. To have quality data, the data-collection instruments, among other things, should be designed in a careful and systematic way. The researcher has to answer the following questions before deciding the type of data-collection instrument needed and prior to outlining the specific elements to be included in the instrument:

1) *What type of data do I need to answer the research inquiry?* In research, data are collected with a purpose to answer specific research questions. In other words, the nature or type of the data collected should allow the researcher to answer his or her research questions. Some research questions can be answered with numeric (quantitative) data from a large number of research participants; others may require in-depth interaction with or observation of a few research participants, often in their natural settings (qualitatively). Still other research inquiry may require a combination of both (mixed).

2) *Where do I get the data or information?* Data should be collected from the source—when possible from primary sources but also from secondary sources. The researcher needs to identify the source of the data or information. This is very critical. The researcher,

for example, should not assume that everybody in organization ABC can provide reliable and valid information about ABC.

3) *Who will provide me the information needed for the research?* This question is about understanding the individuals who can provide the needed information. In research terms, this has to do with understanding the nature of participants of the study. The participants' level of education, their role or position, their availability and willingness to provide the needed data, and their level of understanding of the information needed are very important. If participants of the study, for example, do not understand English, interviewing in English or asking them to fill a questionnaire written in the English language will be inappropriate. In short, the researcher needs to have at least a general or cursory knowledge about potential research participants.

4) *How do I get the information?* After the researcher knows the source and understands the nature of the research participants, the next step will be to think about the best or realistic way to get the needed information. If the study requires information from hundreds and thousands of individuals, for example, one-on-one interview might not be the best or most feasible way to collect data.

5) *Do I have any other way to get the needed information?* Sometimes, the researcher may not need to collect new data to conduct his or her research. A historical researcher may get better information from archival, historical data, rather than through collecting new data

through interviews or questionnaires. It is also wise to see if legitimate raw data is out there for you to use rather than reinventing the wheel. The National Center for Education Statistics (NCES), for example, regularly collects data in a wide range of topics in education and allows researchers to freely use their raw data for educational purposes. The researcher may benefit from such data sets as long as they help to effectively address the purpose of the research.

After the researcher answered these questions, which go hand in hand with making decisions of the intended research design for the study, the next step will be content mapping.

Content Mapping

Content mapping is a process of deciding the needed content and aligning it with the intended purpose. To do so, the researcher needs to have a good background knowledge of what is to be studied and the purpose of the study. By the time the researcher is planning to design the data-collection instrument, it is expected that he or she has already intensively reviewed literature on the topic, including the methodologies used in prior studies. Specifically, under normal circumstance, the researcher has already completed the draft research proposal that includes review of the related literature along with the purpose statement and research questions, which are critical for content mapping.

Content mapping requires outlining a logical linkage between *the research topic, research questions, and the intended contents/items for the instrument.* Without having a clear view of the connection of these three, designing effective data-collection instruments will be extremely challenging and at times frustrating.

The following example will help to illustrate the process of content mapping. Let us say a researcher wants to study "Factors behind dysfunctional organizations" and wants to explore this topic using four research questions:

1) Does leadership play a role in organizational dysfunction?

2) What contributions do employees make for organizational dysfunction?

3) What role does the organizational culture play for organizational dysfunction?

4) What is the impact of governance and organizational structure on organizational dysfunction?

To answer each research question above, the researcher needs to have a list of intended content areas that will help to design more specific questions such as interview or questionnaire items. Table 3 below illustrates the link between research topic, research questions, and possible content to design specific items.

Table 3 *The link between research topic, research questions, and content*

Research topic/title	Research questions	Contents/possible items for data-collection tools (such as for questionnaire and interview)
Factors behind dysfunctional organizations	1) Does leadership play a role in organizational dysfunction?	Specific items related to leadership:
	2) What contributions do employees make for organizational dysfunction?	Specific items related to employees
	3) What role does the organizational culture play for organizational dysfunction?	Specific items related to organizational culture
	4) What is the impact of governance and organizational structure on organizational dysfunction?	Specific items related to governance and structure

Note: See a sample questionnaire (Sample A) at the end of this section, designed based on the above example that addresses Research Question 1 (leadership).

Decision on the Type of Data-Collection Instrument for a Study

As the name suggests, instruments are tools. They are useful for the purpose they are intended to serve but they are nothing on their own. In research, data-collection tools are designed to serve the purpose of the research. The type of data-collection instrument to be used for the study is, therefore, determined based on the research methodology or design of the study. Data for qualitative research design, for example, are collected using interview or observation while quantitative research design requires numeric data usually collected using questionnaire or survey instrument. The decision on selecting the instrument type for your study is as simple as this. However, constructing items of the data-collection instrument that serves the purpose of the study needs more thinking, thorough understanding of the subject matter and the participants, and a good knowledge of designing questions. In the following sections, I will discuss specific data-collection instruments commonly used in education and social sciences, namely, the questionnaire, interview protocol, and observation instrument.

Questionnaire Design

A questionnaire is used to collect numeric data from a relatively large number of individuals. In research, a questionnaire is designed to collect valid and reliable data from participants with the purpose of using the data to help answer the research inquiry or questions posed by the researcher. To serve such a purpose, the questionnaire has to be carefully designed and administered. Here are some valuable considerations for designing a good questionnaire.

1. *Relevance of Items*: It is frustrating for a researcher to collect data and later to find out that the data collected do not help to answer some important research questions. To avoid such commonly made mistake, the researcher needs to thoroughly plan and think about each research question vis-à-vis items of the questionnaire. In short, items to be included in the questionnaire need to be relevant to the research. One way of ensuring this is through content mapping, which was explained earlier. Content mapping helps not only to include items needed to be included but also to exclude irrelevant ones.

2. *Size*: The other very important element that needs utmost attention is the length of the questionnaire. A questionnaire should not be unreasonably long or short. How long or how short may not be determined by anyone's opinion, including this author's. It all depends on the nature of the study and the type of participants—*one size does*

not fit all! While a questionnaire should be exhaustive enough to address research questions, it shouldn't be extremely long to discourage research participants from full participation. Similarly, extremely short questionnaires prohibit the researcher from asking sufficient questions and ultimately impede effective analysis of data. The bottom line—balance! Based on experience, the rule of thumb I usually give to my students is to limit their questionnaire to a maximum of twenty minutes. Remember—you are asking participants a favor and that should not be too much of their time.

3. *Participants*: A questionnaire should take into account the research participants in many ways. First, the questions should be easily understood by the participants. Hence, avoiding unnecessary jargons and technical terms is crucial. Second, the information asked should be something the participants (if possible all participants) could answer off their head, without referring to any document or without doing any additional home work.

4. *Item Types*: Broadly speaking, items could be framed either as closed-ended (structured) or open-ended (unstructured). There are advantages and disadvantages to each type of design. Open-ended questions are more time consuming both for the research participants and the researcher. Unless the researcher has a special reason to include open-ended questions, such as difficulty of asking the specific question in a closed-ended type, a quantitative researcher is advised to minimize the use of open-ended questions. Closed-ended questions

come in many forms ranging from dichotomous such as yes/no to multiple choice, rank order, and scaled type. *The type of item impacts the type of data-analysis techniques to be used.* An item that is framed in a categorical way, for example, cannot be analyzed the same way as those framed in a continuous way. The researcher, therefore, needs to think about the analysis technique to be used as he or she constructs the items.

5. *Item Parts:* The first section of a questionnaire explains the purpose of the research, institutional affiliation of the researcher, and introduces the questionnaire itself among other things. The items are at least grouped in two parts. All background questions such as experience, gender, educational background, and other questions relevant to the research are asked in one part (usually as part 1, but some put this as the last part). The rest of the questions could be grouped in one or more groups depending on the type and focus of the questions. Usually, items that inquire aspects of a single issue or variable are put in one group. Using our prior example of *dysfunctional organization*, all items related to *leadership* can be grouped together; the same can be done with the rest of the three variables. (See "Sample A" at the end of this section.)

6. *Item Sequence*: Items need to be sequenced in some kind of logical order. Typical questionnaire items could be sequenced in what is called either funnel or inverted-funnel manners (Parasuraman, Grewal, & Krishnan, 2004). As the depictions suggest, the funnel

sequence type begins with the general type question and gradually narrows to specific type questions. The opposite is true for the inverted-funnel sequence-type items. Not all items fit into such sequencing. Sometimes the logical way to sequence could be based on relatedness of item contents; other times it could be based on the level of sensitivity. It is up to the researcher to decide the sequence based on what makes sense for the purpose of the research.

7. *Item per page:* Another technical aspect of designing a questionnaire is on the number of items per page. There is no simple and direct answer for this. The type of items and the length of questions need to be factored. Scaled-type questions, for example, are relatively short and easy to answer; multiple choice questions or open-ended items, on the other hand, could be a bit lengthy and time taking. It is therefore better to think in terms of time than item number. Five minutes' worth of question per page may be a reasonable amount.

8. *Mode:* There are two common types of quantitative data-collection mechanisms via questionnaire: *paper and pencil* and *electronic/online*. Each has its advantages and disadvantages. Paper and pencil questionnaire may be useful to collect data from people who have no or limited Internet access. As long as participants have access to the Internet, an electronic questionnaire is better for various reasons. An electronic questionnaire reaches participants in an instance and the responses of participants are automatically entered to the database, thereby saving the researcher's time and energy in entering data manually.

Sample A: A Sample Questionnaire

Note: This questionnaire is based on the Content Mapping, indicated in Table 3, and it covers only research question 1. The items in this questionnaire thus address only questions related to *Leadership*.

Introduction

Thank you for being a part of this study. Your response is very important to the study. This survey has two major parts. Part I is a brief background about the research participant. Part II contains questions that ask participants to rate organizational functionality. The survey will take approximately ten minutes. By filling this survey you are consenting to participate in the study. This study is anonymous, meaning your identity is not known to the researcher and data is reported in aggregate. Again, your participation is much appreciated.

Part I: Background of Participants

Instruction: Choose that better/best describes you from the given alternatives.

1. Your gender
   a. Male
   b. Female
2. You currently work for
   a. Government /public (local, state, federal…)
   b. For-profit (small business, corporation…)
   c. Nonprofit/nongovernmental
      (foundations/religious/charity/community based…)
3. Your overall professional work experience
   a. 1–5 years
   b. 6–10 years
   c. 11–20 years
   d. 21 years and over
4. Your supervisory experience (if you supervised two or more individuals and specified job functions as your formal job responsibilities).
   a. 1–5 years

    b.   6–10 years

    c.   11 years and over

    d.   None

5. Your educational status/highest degree

    a.   High-school diploma

    b.   Some college coursework/associate degree

    c.   Undergraduate degree

    d.   Master's degree

    e.   Doctoral/terminal degree

    f.   Other, please specify_____

PART II: Organization-Related Questions

Instruction: Think of any organization that you know close enough to rate its leader, staff, and the way business is done in the organization and the governance practices in general. This organization could be your previous or current workplace. Let's call this organization/institution X. First let's establish the level of functionality of institution X according to your overall judgment.

6. How would do you rate X as an organization in a scale of 1 to 9 where:

1 = Extremely dysfunctional, 9 = Very well functioning

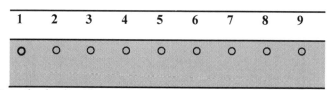

7. Rate the leader (the person who is at the helm of the organization or that heads a division/unit) in organization X.

Indicate your agreement to the statements about the organization below, based on your judgment in a scale of 1 to 9, where: 1 = Not at all descriptive and 9 = Very descriptive.

Item	1	2	3	4	5	6	7	8	9
a. The leader is genuine and truly devoted to the organization's goals/cause.	O	O	O	O	O	O	O	O	O
b. The leader has a comprehensive knowledge about the organization and its functions (he or she is well informed and understands trends and new technologies appropriate to the field).	O	O	O	O	O	O	O	O	O
c. The leader has rich leadership experience.	O	O	O	O	O	O	O	O	O
d. The leader has rich job experience relevant to the organization.	O	O	O	O	O	O	O	O	O
e. The leader understands well the overall environment (political, social, economic) and the community in which the organization operates.	O	O	O	O	O	O	O	O	O
f. The leader often exhibits good judgment in the timing and appropriateness of critical decisions/actions needed.	O	O	O	O	O	O	O	O	O
g. The leader is skillful in working with people (all stakeholders).	O	O	O	O	O	O	O	O	O
h. The leader is visionary.	O	O	O	O	O	O	O	O	O
i. The leader is persistent and tenacious, even at tough times.	O	O	O	O	O	O	O	O	O
j. The leader does not usually seek spotlight but rather acknowledges team efforts. He or she prefers to serve rather than to be served.	O	O	O	O	O	O	O	O	O
k. Under his or her leadership, the organization has been consistently meeting the goals set.	O	O	O	O	O	O	O	O	O
l. The leader is willing to learn or to change when situations demand.	O	O	O	O	O	O	O	O	O
m. The leader practices what he or she preaches and is a good role model.	O	O	O	O	O	O	O	O	O
n. The leader motivates and cultivates others to grow as leaders.	O	O	O	O	O	O	O	O	O
o. The leader meets ethical expectation required by the position/job.	O	O	O	O	O	O	O	O	O
p. The leader usually brings unique and productive insight in discussions and problem-solving strategies.	O	O	O	O	O	O	O	O	O
q. All in all, the leader is highly effective	O	O	O	O	O	O	O	O	O

Note: This is part of a questionnaire that addresses only the "leadership" items.

Designing the Interview Protocol

The interview is the most widely used data-collection instrument for qualitative research. As stated earlier, the choice of a specific data-collection instrument is decided before the researcher is ready to collect data. Once the interview is decided to be the tool to collect the intended data, the researcher needs to develop the protocol for interviewing.

An interview protocol is basically a written format to be used by the interviewer that outlines and documents the data-collection procedure from start to finish. While each protocol may differ, by and large, a good format comprises several specific components. A comprehensive form will have the following specific parts.

The first part of the protocol documents *basic information* including the following: place, date, and time of the interview; name and title of the interviewee; institutional affiliation of the interviewee; and name of the interviewer. Additional information such as demographic background about the participant and any relevant preinterview notes by the interviewer may be added here. This section is very important, whether the interview is going to be recorded or not. It helps the researcher to accurately document data in an organized manner.

In addition, when writing the report, according to APA format, the researcher is expected to cite some basic information like the date and the name (pseudonym) of the interviewee. Thus, documenting complete basic-information data is crucial.

Part 2 of the protocol provides *instructions for the interviewer.* The instructions are basically scripts that the interviewer will do or say right before starting to ask the interview questions. The script addresses many important elements. It states who the researcher is, explains the purpose of the meeting, thanks the interviewee for the time, provides an estimate on how many minutes the interview will take, describes the manner in which the interview is recorded, and confirms their agreement/consent to be interviewed on the spot. Additional details such as issues of consent, confidentiality, and rights of participants should be added as outlined in the study's approved IRB application. The script also explains the procedure of the interview, as a transition to the interview questions. Depending of the nature of the study, additional contents could be added to the script.

Part 3 of the form contains five to eight *interview questions.* The form will have sufficient space between questions for the interviewer to take down notes. When appropriate probing or follow-up questions are stated under each question. Some advice on designing interview questions is discussed in a separate section below.

The last part of the interview protocol/form is the *closing* section. This is where the researcher thanks the research participant and provides some information regarding the next step of the research process such as member checking, which is asking if the participant will be interested in reviewing the analysis of the study before it goes public. In addition, a space for postinterview notes is provided for the researcher to write some general points he or she believes is important for the study. A sample interview protocol ("Sample B") is provided at the end of this section.

Advice on Constructing Interview Questions

Behind any well-written qualitative research, there is always a good set of interview questions. Interview questions are the keys that unlock the needed "treasure" for research *data*. Constructing interview items, therefore, demands a careful and thoughtful effort from the researcher. The following elements will help to guide the construction of interview questions.

1. Relevance: As discussed in the content-mapping section of this chapter, any instrument (including interview items) is utterly useless unless it is aligned to answer the main inquiry the researcher intends to answer. Interview items need to be carefully constructed to garner as much relevant or rich information as possible to enable the researcher to get an in-depth understanding about the phenomenon being studied. All research questions need to have one or more corresponding interview question(s). There shouldn't be any interview question that is not linked to the research questions.

2. Amount: Novice researchers are often tempted to ask as many questions as they can, to get "as much information as possible." In research, the amount of information is determined, by and large, by the scope and the purpose of the study. Even when the researcher is focused within the scope and the purpose of the study, the number of interview questions matter at least for two reasons. First, the interviewee is doing the researcher a favor, so the researcher needs to be considerate enough to their time. Second, many questions mean more time (or fewer minutes per item). Both of these reasons could inadvertently limit the quality of information you collect. Although there is no magic number, interview questions should be between six and ten.

3. Type: The type of interview questions affect the type of information collected. Open-ended questions are usually the preferred type of questions to collect data via interview. However, the way open-ended questions are framed also matters. For example, questions that ask the "how" encourage the interviewee to share more information than those that ask the "what." While asking "what" questions is sometimes unavoidable, the researcher needs to construct such questions in such a way that they won't discourage the interviewee from providing the needed information. Questions that begin with "What do you think about XYZ?" for example, generate better data than "What is your take on XYZ?"

4. Tone: An interview is conducted for various reasons. Conducting an interview for research is different from job interview or journalistic interview. While the interviewer may grill during interviews in the latter cases, the research interview should be more sensitive in approach. The tone of both the scripted questions and the interviewer should be one of respect, because the researcher is at the mercy of the interviewees for their data. This doesn't mean the researcher shouldn't ask investigative questions if the nature of the study demands. It only means that the tone should not indicate a sense of disrespect or suspicion. In addition, avoid any ideologically or politically charged statement verbally or in script as this could limit the type of information you receive.

5. Clear and Crisp: Interview questions should be brief and to the point. Avoid long and ambiguous questions. Also avoid jargon and clichés. The questions also should not be suggestive, biased, or double barreled. Suggestive questions provide possible answers in the question, thereby influencing the interviewee to support the suggested claims. Double-barreled questions pack more than one issue in a single question, which makes it difficult for the interviewee to provide a concrete or focused answer.

6. Uniformity: All interviewees should be asked the same questions in a similar manner. Thus, the researcher needs to make sure that the questions are at the level where all participants can answer. This takes, more than any other things, knowing the research participants.

7. Probe: Follow-up questions are needed for three major reasons. First, the interviewee may have touched a relevant issue that needs more explanation or clarifications. Second, if the interviewee for some reason missed the essence of the question, the researcher may have felt it necessary to redirect a question. Third, the nature of the question needs probing by design; in which case, the researcher is well prepared in advance to probe interviewees who answered a certain question in a certain way. Follow-up questions provide flexibility for the researcher to make sure optimal responses are collected, and the focus of the interview is maintained.

8. Sequence: Qualitative research usually explores one central phenomenon. Interview questions are designed to explore segments or pieces of the central phenomenon in order to fully explore the core of the matter. These questions, for the most part, are interrelated. A conscious planning on the sequence of the questions helps to receive a steady flow of ideas from the interviewees. The researcher, therefore, needs to make sure a logical order of questioning is followed during the interview.

9. Mode: Interviews may be organized in various formats. While a face-to-face interview is the most common one, interviews can be conducted using various technologies such as phone, the Internet, or other video conferencing mechanisms. In any case, it is recommended that the conversation to be live interaction since that allows follow-up or additional probing questions. Before you resort to the non-face-to-face medium, there needs to be a convincing reason to do so. A mere convenience should not be the motivation.

Sample B: A Sample Interview Protocol

Topic: Implications of Organizational practices on Organizational Functions

I. Basic Information

1. Place of Interview_____

2. Date of Interview_____

3. Time of Interview: Started at_____Ended at _____

4. Interviewee's:

      i.   Name_____,

      ii. Title_____

      iii. Institutional Affiliation_____

5. Interviewer's Name_____

II. Instruction for Interviewer

Protocol Script:

Thank you for the time and your willingness to speak with me today. The interview will take approximately an hour and it will be audio recorded. The audio data will not be accessible to any person except this researcher. After transcription, the audio data will be destroyed. The transcription and the subsequent data-analysis document will use pseudonym to maintain confidentiality of your identity.

Before we proceed with the interview, you need to sign these documents that you understand and agree. Participation is voluntary, you can withdraw from the study at any time with no ramifications to you, and the study is confidential.

Introduction Script

The purpose of this study is to get deeper understanding of organizational practices and its implications on organizational functions. I have six interview questions that touch various aspects of organizational practices. Organizational practice, for this research, is defined as the predominant way of doing business in an organization.

III. Interview Questions

1) What mechanisms does the institution use to improve or enhance organizational performance?

2) How do you describe the working relationship of employees in the organization?

3) How do you see the reward and promotion mechanism of the organization?

4) How are relevant decisions made in the organization?

5) How do you describe the use of resources (time, human, material, and financial) in the organization?

6) How does the organization perform compared to other institutions or peers?

IV. Closing

Script: I have concluded my questions. Thank you for your time again. When I complete the draft data analysis, I plan to share it with my research participants so that they can check how their views are presented before it goes public. Will you be interested in receiving the draft data analysis and providing feedback accordingly?

Closing Note:

Designing Observation Instruments

Marshall and Rossman (1989) defined observation as "the systematic description of events, behaviors, and artifacts in the social setting chosen for study" (p.79). Data collection through observation is a widely used approach in various fields of studies to conduct qualitative research. Qualitative researchers in social sciences and humanities spend a considerable amount of time with research participants to be able to get firsthand accounts about the issue being studied as it unfolds in the natural setting.

Not all qualitative studies are the same. Some studies more than others require the researcher to be fluent in his or her understanding of the culture or the context in which the study is conducted to minimize a possible misinterpretation of data. Observation is the preferred data-collection instrument among ethnographic researchers because familiarity with culture and to context is of utmost importance for such studies.

Observation can be made in a variety of ways using various approaches. Here are some features of observation:

1. *Visibility: Overt or Covert?* Observation data may be collected openly or secretly depending on the purpose of the study. In the case of the overt observation, the participants know who the researcher is and the purpose of his or her presence. An example of overt observation could be a researcher observing a classroom where he or

she is obviously known by the students and the teacher. Covert observation involves secrecy and is commonly known by IRB as "deception studies." While deception studies could be structured in various ways, one example is when the researcher secretly collects observation data from participants. A carefully planned observation data collection that takes a form of "mystery shopper" or "undercover agent" falls under this category.

2. *Involvement: Participant Observation or Direct Observation?* Participant observation is a qualitative data collection approach in which the researcher participates in the experience, the culture, and the context being observed while collecting observation data. Participant observation is more appropriate in cultural studies such as anthropology and sociology. In the case of direct observation, the researcher detaches self from the experience as he or she collects observation data. Direct observers pay utmost attention not to interrupt any experience by being as less noticeable or inconspicuous as possible.

3. *Setting: Natural or Controlled?* While observation for qualitative research in humanities and social sciences usually takes place in the natural or real-life setting, there are times when researchers use controlled or artificial settings for observation. Example of observation in natural setting could be observing teachers in their classrooms. Observation in controlled setting, for example, could be observing employees performing tasks that are not part of their regular task, in an artificially designed setting by the researcher.

4. *Period: Extended or Brief?* Depending on the purpose of the research, observation data collection may take short windows of time or extended periods of time. Sometimes the researcher's continued and extended observation is critical, such as in the case of cultural study or an ethnography, because understanding the culture is very critical for interpretation of the data. In addition, if the purpose of the study is to document a process with a clear or definite beginning and end, the researcher may need to observe the entire process for the duration of the process. But in most other cases, the researcher may need a few, but critical, windows of time to observe.

5. *Design: Quantitative or Qualitative?* Usually observation in social sciences and humanities is used for qualitative or mixed-methods designs. In rare instances, observation is used for quantitative data collection such as to observe repeated occurrences. Let's say a researcher wants to document distractive student behaviors in a classroom. Through tallying the occurrences by gender and by the type of behavior every time they happen, a quantitative researcher may use the data for quantitative analysis.

6. *Recording: Manual or Technology?* Depending on the nature of the study and the approval of the relevant IRB, observation data could be recorded in three different ways. The customary traditional approach is for the researcher to be physically present and document the observation. The second approach is to video record the entire experience for watching it at a convenient time. The third approach is

to live-stream the experience as it progresses for the researcher to observe it from distance via webcam or surveillance cameras.

7. *Amount: Entire or Partial?* While human limitations are understood, observation data need to be as complete as possible. There is no such thing as irrelevant or trivial information when it comes to observation. When conversations happen, for example, verbatim recording is highly encouraged. Rich description of the environment in which the targeted observation occurs and the individuals involved is essential as well. At the time of writing the research report, the researcher will be able to carefully select what to include and not to include in the research document.

Types of Observation Instruments

Observation data can be collected in various ways depending on the purpose of the study. The instrument type to be used for a study is also dictated by the purpose of the observation. There are at least three categories of observation tools used by researchers. Each is discussed below.

i. *Structured Observation Tool*: This is a predesigned instrument similar to questionnaire to be filled by the researcher. The structured tool usually contains a list of items to be checked or filled by the researcher at the time of observation. The researcher comes prepared knowing what to observe and all he or she does is document the occurrences of the expected actions or happenings. See a sample structured observation instrument used to observe classroom teaching

("Sample C. i") at the end of this section.

ii.   *Semistructured Observation Tool*: This is similar to an unstructured interview in a sense that the researcher is guided by a specific set of parameters or questions in an open-ended manner. However, the researcher is not necessarily directly interacting with the participant like in an interview. The questions are guides to the researcher, not directed to participants to respond. Unlike structured observation, the researcher in semistructured observation doesn't come with expected possible answers to check or tally. Rather, the researcher documents what he or she observes vis-à-vis the prepared open-ended questions. See a sample semistructured observation instrument used to observe classroom teaching ("Sample C. ii") at the end of this section.

iii.   *Unstructured Observation Tool*: This is the most flexible observation tool to gather rich data for qualitative research. Unstructured observation is not guided by preset questions or parameters. The researcher is free to record whatever he or she observes during the time of observation. The primary mode of recording of unstructured observation could be one or more of the following: video, audio, summarized field notes, verbatim notes (if the observation involves conversation), sketching, still pictures, and other artifacts. Note taking is always recommended even though the researcher uses other primary mode of recordings. See a sample unstructured observation instrument ("Sample C. iii") at the end of this section.

Sample C: Sample Observation Instruments

C. i. A Sample *Structured* Observation Instrument

Place of Observation_____

Name of Observer _____

What/Who Is Observed?_____

Date of Observation_____

Time of Observation: Started_____ Ended_____

Checklist for Teacher Observation (*not intended for actual use*)

Items/Activities	Yes	No	Comment
1. Used lesson plan			
2. Summarized previous lesson			
3. Introduced the day's lesson			
4. Demonstrated a good command of the subject matter/lesson covered			
5. Delivered the subject matter with clarity			
6. Used appropriate audiovisual teaching aid/technology			
7. All students were engaged/no student or group was left out			
8. Teacher didn't talk too much			
9. Encouraged students			
10. Gave controlled class activity			

11. Provided appropriate feedback/ correction			
12. Summarized the day's lesson			
13. Used the time effectively			
14. Managed the class well			
15. Provided homework			
16. Briefly introduced the next lesson			

C. ii: A Sample *Semistructured* Observation Instrument Items

Place of Observation_____

Name of Observer _____

What/Who Is Observed?_____

Date of Observation_____

Time of Observation: Started_____ ended_____

1. Introduction of the Lesson:

2. Presentation of the Lesson:

3. Method of Lesson Delivery:

4. Interaction with Students:

5. Mastery of the Lesson or Subject Matter:

6. Closing of the Lesson:

7. Organization of the Lesson:

C. iii: A Sample *Unstructured* Observation

For Field Note and Verbatim

Place of Observation_____

Name of Observer _____

What/Who Is Observed?_____

Date of Observation_____

Time of Observation: Started_____ Ended_____

*Note*_____

_____

_____

_____

_____

_____

_____

_____

_____

_____

_____

Testing of Data Collection Instruments

Before using the instruments for data collection, the researcher needs to test the validity and reliability of the instrument. The objective is to improve the quality of the instrument. The following two steps are usually followed to maximize the quality of the data-collection instrument: pretesting and pilot testing.

Pretesting

Pretest is done through sharing the instrument to small number of individuals from two groups: (1) expert group and (2) potential target group. The expert group includes five to eight individuals who have a content knowledge of the issue/content to be studied. If the study is about *mental health*, professionals in the field of mental health will help to provide feedback on the relevance and completeness of contents to improve the quality of the instrument. The potential target group includes individuals of similar background to the intended participants, but who are not part of the study. Information from potential target group will help to improve the appropriateness and understandability of the questions in the instrument. If the participants of the research are teachers in school A, the target group may be teachers recruited from school B. Once the instrument is improved accordingly, the next step will be pilot testing.

Pilot testing

Pilot testing, as Vogt and Johnson (2011, p. 290) noted, is "dress rehearsal of a research project." It is conducted in a small size sample of actual study participants before the study is conducted full scale. Pilot testing has two major purposes. Primarily it helps to "catch" potential undetected issues during the design and pretesting of the instrument. By so doing, it helps to avoid the risk of wasting resources in a larger scale.

Part 3:

Common Dissertation Terminologies and Concepts

This section comprises research terminologies that any person writing a dissertation might want to familiarize self. They are presented in three subsections: general dissertation terminologies, quantitative research terminologies, and qualitative research terminologies. While these may seem elementary for some, they are often misused by many.

General Dissertation Terminologies and Concepts

Annotated Bibliography: Is a bibliographical list of relevant resources/literature (books, articles, documents) complied by a researcher. It provides not only the reference information but also summary of the study in a paragraph or so describing its quality and relevance to the intended research.

Claim: Statements made by the researcher for the readers to believe. Example "Students in School ABC achieved very high compared to their peers in similar schools nationwide."

Dissertation Chair/Advisor: The dissertation chair advises the candidate from the inception of the research idea to the completion of the work. This person in most traditional higher education institutions is chosen by the individual candidate while some institutions assign a chair. Most institutions follow a "strong chair model" where the chair advises the candidate on who to invite to the dissertation committee, organizes the proposal and oral defense, and presides over the approval decision of the candidate's work.

Dissertation Committee: Traditionally, at the time the candidate is ready to start the dissertation work, a committee of two to five individuals (comprised of faculty members and other professionals external to the candidate's department) is established that guides the candidate research process and evaluates/judges the quality of the work at least at two different junctions: during the proposal defense and oral defense.

Dissertation Defense/Oral Defense: This is the final step in the dissertation process where the candidate presents and defends his or her work before the dissertation committee, usually in a public forum. The committee makes judgment on the candidate's work soon after the defense. The outcome usually takes one of the three: approval, approval with revision, disapproval.

Dissertation Proposal: Before the candidate formally begins the research, he or she prepares a proposal that describes and argues for the intended study. While a proposal format differs from college to college, usually it comprises the entire or most parts of the first three chapters of a dissertation. Many institutions require that the candidate defends the proposal before a committee for approval.

Evidence: Reasons or supporting data why the readers should believe a claim/claims.

Institutional Review Board (IRB): The IRB is the institutional body mandated with ensuring the protection of the right and welfare of human subjects (research participants). Higher education institutions have local institutional IRBs that are responsible in determining whether each research applications/proposals meet the standard before the researcher begins data collection including contacting potential research participants.

Methodologist: As a practice, in education and some social sciences fields, one of the individuals in a dissertation committee will have a stronger expertise in a specific research design or data-analysis technique the candidate uses for his or her dissertation. This person is commonly referred as the methodologist. The methodologist is a close advisor to the candidate next to the dissertation chair.

Population and Sample

Population: The "population is a large group to whom results can be generalized" (McMillan 2012, p.96).

Example: New York State residents; first-year teachers in the United States; first-generation immigrants in Canada.

Sample: "A group of cases or subjects selected from the larger group in the hope that the smaller group (sample) will reveal information about the larger group (the population)" (Vogt and Johnson 2011, p.347).

Note: Ideally, a sample is the miniature of the population it represents.

Research: Research is the search for knowledge through the application of scientific methods. Scientific method relies on empirical and measureable evidence. The process of research involves systematic collection, analyzing, and reporting of data using appropriate research procedure to answer specific research questions.

Research Bias: This term means "anything that produces systematic error of a research finding" (Vogt & Johnson, 2011, p.28). Bias could be reflected through the selection of research participants, such as *including participants that do not reflect the general population* or through the researcher's perception such as studying an issue with a strong opinion to "prove" or "disprove" it. While some types of biases could be inadvertent, other types of biases may involve conflict of interest.

Research Ethics: Is the principle outlined to govern good or bad research practices. Conducting research requires a high level of integrity and respecting regulations that govern the research process. Some of these regulations include: (1) respecting the proprietary rights/intellectual property such as copyrights and (2) protecting the rights and welfare of research participants (subjects).

Research versus Opinion: *Research* is a data-driven process to reach into conclusions, whereas *opinion* is judgment based on personal views or assumptions that lack sufficient ground to produce certainty.

Research Questions versus Research Hypotheses

Research Question: The research question states the problem to be investigated in the form of questions. It is exploratory by nature.

Example: Is there any relationship between class size and student achievement?

Hypothesis: The research problem is written in the form of testable statement or tentative answer. A hypothesis is largely restricted to experimental/quantitative studies; never for qualitative studies. A null hypothesis is a statement that the researcher wants to prove wrong, which is basically the opposite of the hypothesis.

Example:

Hypothesis: There is an inverse relationship between class size and student achievement.

Null Hypothesis: There is no relationship between class size and student achievement.

Significance: Significance is "the degree to which a research finding is meaningful or important" (Vogt & Johnson, 2011, p.360). Significance testing is also called "hypothesis testing."

Types of Research: The types are broadly categorized into three:

1. *Quantitative Research*: A type of research that uses numerical or quantitative data to investigate a research problem with the intent to accurately describe, predict, explain, and experiment. It involves a systematic statistical analysis of the raw data collected. Data is usually collected via questionnaire or survey instruments.

2. *Qualitative Research*: A type of research that utilizes qualitative evidence such as words from interviews, artifacts, and observation, with the purpose of understanding, exploring, explaining, and describing phenomenon.

3. *Mixed Methods*: This type of research is a combination of 1 and 2 above. Researchers use this type of study when they believe the study is better addressed by combining both methods due to the nature of the study. While such a study helps to utilize the strength of the two methods, it adds to the complexity of the research process as it requires more time and managing varied types of data.

Types of Sampling: Broadly categorizing, there are two types of sampling: probability and nonprobability.

Probability Sampling gives known, equal, chance of selection/representation of subjects/participants.

Nonprobability Sampling doesn't give equal chance of selection or representation to individual subjects/participants.

See components of chapter 3 for more detail in sampling strategies.

Units of Analysis: The unit of analysis refers to the targets of the investigation (individuals, groups, or things) about whom data is gathered and analysis is made. If data about schools are gathered, the center of the analysis (the unit of analysis) will be the schools. If the study focuses on school leaders, the data to be collected will be about school leaders, and the unit of analysis will be the "school leaders."

Variables: A variable is any factor or entity that has quantitative or qualitative value that change/vary. Example: age, weight, IQ, salary. *Please see chapter 3 for types of variables.*

Warrant: Relevancy and appropriateness of the evidences for the claims made.

Quantitative Research Terminologies

ANOVA (Analysis of Variance): This analysis is the same as *t*-test; the difference is ANOVA is used when the number of groups is two or MORE.

Chi-square Test: This is a type of statistical test usually conducted when the researcher is interested to know/analyze data in the number of responses per category to see the level of statically significant differences between the observed (actual) and expected frequencies of groups. It is suitable to analyze distributions that are not normal/nonparametric by nature.

Correlation: A correlation is a type of statistical-analysis technique that shows the level/extent of relationships between two or more variables. It doesn't tell cause and effect relationships; it only tells if there is relationship. Correlation can be positive or negative. Positive correlation occurs when an increase in one is also associated with an increase of the other. In negative or inverse correlation, an increase in one is a decrease of the other.

Cross-tabulation (Crosstab): This is a method or way of categorizing frequency distribution in a matrix of row and column table format.

Descriptive Statistics: Descriptive statistics describe the result as it appears; it doesn't allow for prediction. It provides information about conditions, situations, and events that occur in the present. *Example*: frequency, percentage, average, range, mode, median.

Discriminant Analysis: This is a type of statistical data-analysis technique used for the same purpose as regression analysis but for categorical data (*see regression below*).

Experimental Study: Is a type of research where systematic manipulation or treatment is applied on subjects (variables) and the result/effect is observed.

Factor Analysis: This is a statistical method used for a variety of purpose and often used to reduce a large amount of variables into fewer variables or factors. This is often applicable when researchers want to condense a long list of survey item to a few manageable constructs. For example, a list of test scores in math, reading, social studies, science, art, and physical education could be condensed into a construct: "Student Achievement" if analysis of the factors generates intercorrelation of the items.

Inferential Statistics: Inferential statistics enable researchers to make inference/predictions based on the findings. Usually, researchers study a sample to make conclusion or decisions about a larger group (population) or cause and effect relationships or prediction about patterns or possible future occurrences of events. *Example:* regression, ANOVA, ANCOVA, correlation, discriminant function analysis.

Logistic Regression: This serves the same purpose as discriminant analysis but it is more appropriate when the category of the dependent variable is dichotomous such as true/false, yes/no, and agree/disagree.

Measurement Levels: Measurement levels are types of scales that are assigned to describe/quantify attributes of values of variables or constructs. There are four measurement levels:

- **Nominal**: Scales with numerical values that denote assigned names for individual or group values. This is when a researcher assigns numbers for variables as codes, such as *political party affiliation* (1 = Democratic, 2 = Republican, 3 = Independent). The numbers are used as symbols and do not tell amount/quantity. Number 3 (Independent) doesn't mean as three times number 1 (Democratic). This type of rating is not useful to calculate mean or median as it doesn't imply amount and ordering. Nominal scales are used to calculate frequency and mode.

- **Ordinal:** Scales with numerical values that can be rank ordered. Examples include ranking of athletes in their performance in a competition (first, second, third) or ranking levels in terms of skill mastery (1 = Beginners; 2 = Intermediate; 3 = Advanced). The order indicates direction. Such ratings are used in calculating median and are used for nonparametric tests.

- **Interval**: Scales with numerical values that are not only ordered but also the scale denote equal intervals. Common examples of interval scores include hours of the day and temperature scales. There are twenty-four hours in a day; as the difference between 7:00 a.m. and 8:00 a.m., for example, is one hour, so is the difference between 10:00 p.m. and 11:00 p.m. The same is true for temperature scales, where the difference between sixty and seventy degrees is the same as the difference between twenty and thirty degrees. Interval scales are used to calculate measures of central tendency (mean, mode, median) and dispersion (range, deviation, variance).

- **Ratio:** Scales with numerical values with a meaningful absolute value of zero. In ratio, zero denotes absence or nonexistence. For example, ratio variables like zero weight, zero children, zero experience are all meaningful and all tell nonexistence unlike zero degree Celsius temperature, where zero is arbitrary. Ratio scales are used to calculate coefficients and mean.

Meta-analysis: A statistical data-analysis technique where data/findings from a large number of similar but independent past research studies are pooled to produce an overall result.

Nonparametric Statistics: When the data to be analyzed does not follow the parameter of the distribution or the population, it is referred as nonparametric or parameter-free. Data with nominal and ordinal measurement scales are usually used to analyze such data. Nonparametric uses Median as a central tendency measure (thereby minimizing the effect of outlier scores).

Parametric Statistics: In quantitative research, when the data has certain characteristics such as when the distribution is normal (ratio, interval), it is considered parametric. It uses mean as a *central* tendency measure.

Pretest-Posttest: Is a type of experimental research usually conducted to study the effect of a treatment or intervention by studying the before (pretest) and after (posttest) treatment differences.

Regression: This is a statistical method used to estimate or predict the value of one group of variables (dependent variables) based on knowledge of another group of variables (independent variables). It is usually conducted to explain or determine impact between variables. Unlike correlation, this one tells causation.

Standard Deviation: This statistic is the distance of scores from the mean, in average. Also known as "deviation from the mean."

***t*-test:** This is a significance test usually to compare the average/mean of two groups.

A researcher may use a *t*-test to compare, for example, to find "if there is any difference in Math achievement between Section 1A and Section 1B due to difference in the teaching method."

Qualitative Research Terminologies

Artifact/Document Review: This is a qualitative data-analysis process, usually done to conduct historical study. It could be formal such as accessing official documents or nonformal by collecting documents such as pictures, materials, diaries. Artifacts and documents are also sometimes used to supplement data from interview or observation.

Coding: In qualitative research, *Code* means "words/phrases that signify data" (McMillan, 2012, p.298). Codes are usually chosen or created by the researcher. Codes are core words or phrases that represent the relevant message from a set of information. Coding helps the researcher to condense a very bulky interview/observation document into organized, categorized, and meaningful data. See Appendix B for more detail.

Field Notes: The notes taken by the researcher during observation, which will serve as data for analysis.

Focus Group Interview: A method of qualitative data collection through interviewing purposefully selected research participants in a group. The panel of the interviewee ranges from six to ten individuals and the researcher/interviewer moderates the Q and A.

Interview: This is the most frequently used method of data collection in qualitative studies.

The interviewer collects and records data by asking questions related to the research/study.

The interview could be face-to-face, via phone, via or video call such as Skype or Google chat; it may be electronically or manually recorded through note taking, video, or audio recording.

Member Checking: Sharing summary of draft data/analysis with research participants for validation purpose.

Observation: A qualitative data-collection method where data is collected and recorded by watching participants. There are two major ways of doing observation: (1) by visiting the research site/participants in action in one or more occasions (short term, cross-sectional by nature) and (2) by being in a site for extended time, participating in the day-to-day work of the participants (most common in ethnography/cultural studies).

Organizing Qualitative Data: The process of getting qualitative data ready for analysis. If audio/video recording is used, everything should be transcribed (changed from audio to written document) verbatim. The researcher or a bond-transcriber may do the transcription. There are also some electronic transcription software programs such as "Transcribe me!"

Themes/Category: In qualitative study, themes are ideas or concepts that represent coded data. See Appendix B for further detail.

Transcription: A written form or typed copies of audio/video recorded data.

Triangulation: Using multiple (two or more) sources or methods to investigate and analyze the same problem.

References

APA Manual. (2009). *Publication Manual of the American Psychological Association.* Washington, DC: American Psychological Association.

Bacharach, S. B. (1989). Organizational theories: Some criteria for evaluation. *Academy of Management Review,* 14(4), 496-515.

Council for Graduate School (2008). *Ph.D. Completion and Attrition: Analysis of Baseline Demographic Data from the Ph.D. Completion Project.* Retrieved on February 19, 2016 from http://www.phdcompletion.org/information/book2.asp

Creswell, J. W. (2009). *Research design: qualitative, quantitative, and mixed methods approaches.* Thousand Oaks, CA: Sage Publications.

Creswell, J. W. (2014). *Research Design Qualitative, Quantitative, and Mixed Methods Approaches (4th ed.).* Thousand Oaks, CA: Sage Publications.

Creswell, J.W.(2015).*Educational research: planning, conducting, and evaluating quantitative and qualitative research.* Boston, MA : Pearson.

Fink, A. (2010). *Conducting research literature reviews : from the Internet to paper.* Thousand Oaks, CA: Sage Publications.

Gay, L.R.; Mills,E.M.; and Airasian,P.W.(2009). *Educational research : competencies for analysis and applications.(9th ed).* Upper Saddle River, N.J. : Merrill/Pearson

Gay, L.R.; Mills,E.M.; and Airasian,p.w.(2012). *Educational research : competencies for analysis and applications. (10th ed.).* Boston, MA : Pearson

Lincoln, Y. S., & Guba, E. G. (1986). But is it rigorous? Trustworthiness and authenticity in naturalistic evaluation. *New Directions for Program Evaluation*,(30), 73-84.

Machi , L.A.and McEvoy, B.T. (2009) *The literature review : Six steps to success.* Thousand Oaks, California : Corwin Press.

Marshall, C. and Rossman, G.B. (1989) *Designing qualitative research.* Newbury Park, California : Sage.

McMillan,J.H.(2012). *Educational research : fundamentals for the consumer.(6th ed.).* Boston :Pearson.

Merriam, S. B. (2001). *Qualitative research and case study applications in education.* San Francisco, CA: Jossey-Bass

Parasuraman,A.; Grewal,D.; and Krishnan, R. (2007). *Marketing Research. (2nd ed.).* Boston, MA: Houghton Mifflin Company.

Trochim, W. M. (2006). *The Research Methods Knowledge Base, 2nd Edition.* Retrieved from http://www.socialresearchmethods.net/kb/

Vogt, W. P. (2007). *Quantitative Research Methods for Professionals in Education and Other Fields.* Boston, MA: Pearson/ Allyn & Bacon.

Vogt, P. & Johnson,B.(2011). *Dictionary of Statistics & Methodology : A Nontechnical Guide for the Social Sciences.* Thousand Oaks, California: Sage Publications.

Wang, C. (2004). *Qualitative Variables. In The Sage Encyclopedia of Social Science Research Methods.* (Vol. 1, pp.132-136). Thousand Oaks, CA: Sage Publications.

Yin, R. K. (2013). *Case study research: Design and methods.* Thousand Oaks, CA: Sage publications.

Appendices

Appendix A: Statistical Data-Analysis Decision Tree

Nature of DV	Nature of IV	Assum-ption	Statistical test	Purpose of inquiry	A sample research question
Categorical	Categorical	Nonparametric	Chi-square (for nominal)	Frequency analysis by comparing what is expected and what is observed	Do women and men differ in their preference of hobbies?
			Wilcoxon rank test	Ranks analysis	What is the difference in their health between those who exercise one hour a day and those who don't exercise at all?
	Continuous	Nonparametric	Spearman Rho	Relationship between ranks/two variables	What is the relationship between attending ivy league college and being employed at fortune 500 companies?
			Logistic regression	The effect of Independent variables on Dependent variable	Does increase in salary result in employee job satisfaction?

Appendix A Continued:
Statistical Data-Analysis Decision Tree

Nature of DV	Nature of IV	Assumption	Statistical test	Purpose of inquiry	A sample research question
Continuous	Categorical	Parametric	Independent *t*-test	Mean difference between two groups	Is there any difference in SAT scores between private and public high-school seniors?
			Dependent *t*-test	Within-group Mean Variation	Is there any difference in SAT scores taken before and after attending a test prep workshop?
			ANOVA	Mean difference of more than two groups	Is there any difference in SAT scores between private, public, and charter high-school seniors?
Continuous	Continuous	Parametric	Pearson correlation	Relationship between two or more groups/variables	What is the relationship between income and years of experience?
			Bivariate regression	Impact/influence of one variable (Independent) on another (Dependent)	What is the effect of time spent on homework on student's high stakes test score?
			Multiple regression	Predict the impact/influence of multiple variables (independent) on the outcome/ dependent variable.	Same as bivariate, except multiple independent variables here.

Appendix B: Qualitative Data-Analysis Process

Sample Interview question	Answer/ raw data transcriptions	Codes	Theme/ category	Data analysis
What qualities of your supervisor do you appreciate?	Let's say you recorded ten pages' worth of interview transcriptions from sixteen of your interviewees.	Based on the data, you observed a pattern that most of your interviewees mentioned similar qualities and you coded them as follow: —*Listens* —*Has a sense of humor* —*Gets along well with employees*	Based on the codes, you may come up with a phrase that will be a theme for the mentioned qualities as follow : *Human skills*	The data analysis will detail how the interviewees like the *human skills* of their supervisor (which is the *claim*) by quoting and paraphrasing the answers/expressions of the interviewees (which is the *evidence*), making the argument *warranted.*

Made in the USA
San Bernardino, CA
10 September 2016